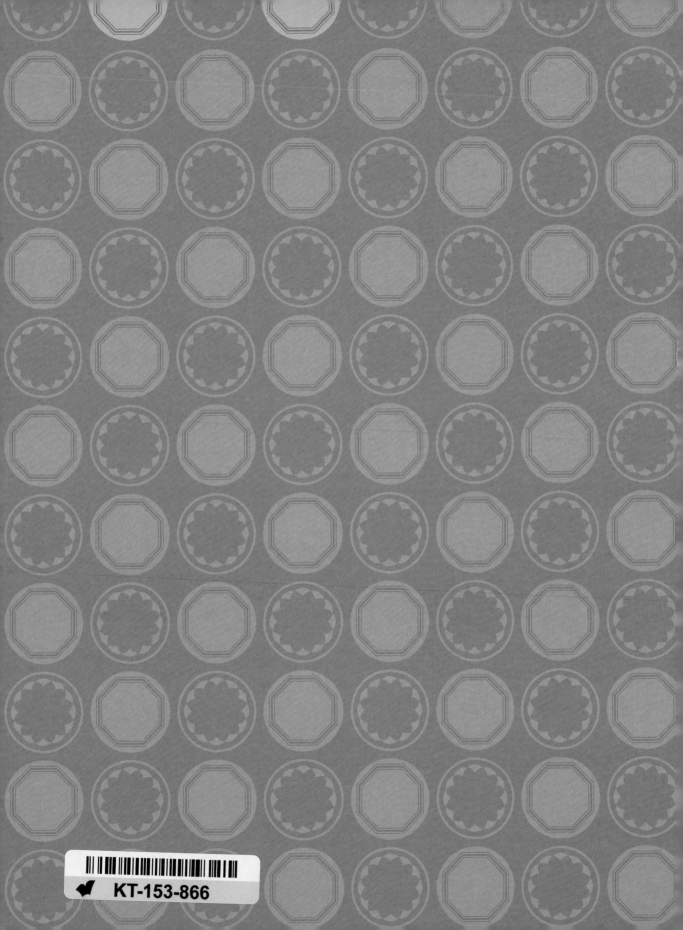

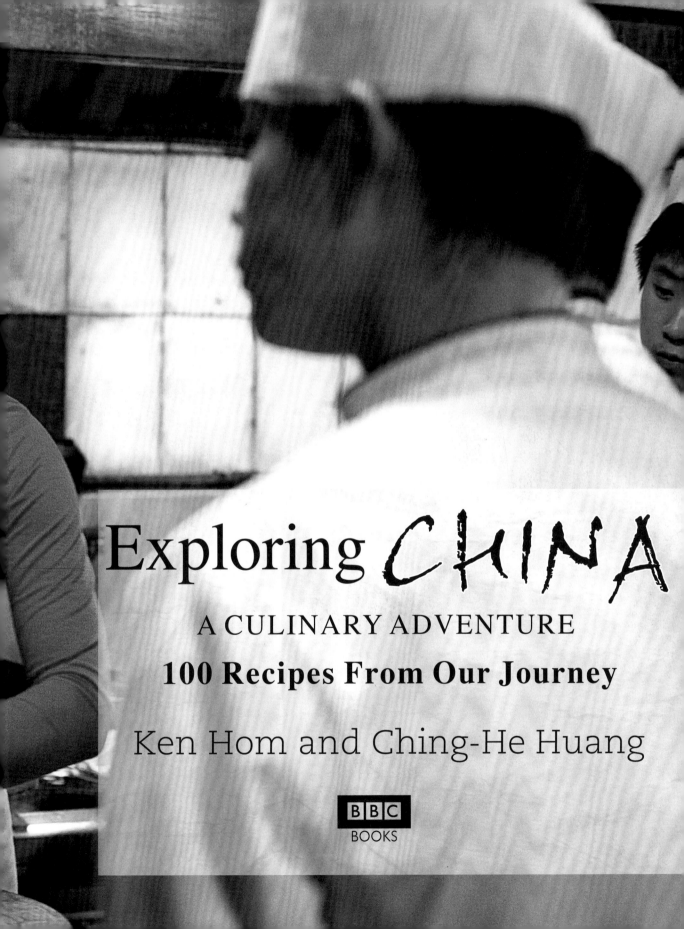

Exploring CHINA

A CULINARY ADVENTURE

100 Recipes From Our Journey

Ken Hom and Ching-He Huang

BBC
BOOKS

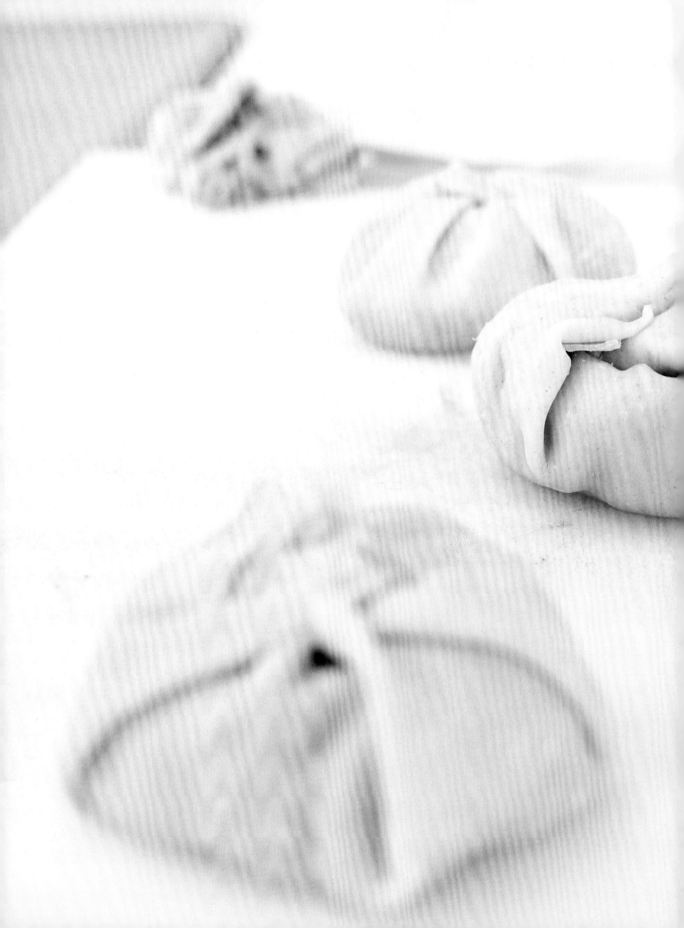

CONTENTS

I don't think there could have been a better time to explore China than when we went, at the beginning of 2012. The real China still exists, thank goodness, even though westernisation and relentless progress are nibbling away at the old traditional ways of doing things, of cooking food, of eating, of thinking, of living. We travelled from the wild frontiers of the north to the industrial megacities of the south and saw the inevitable conflicts between tradition and modernity, between communism and capitalism. But we also talked to the 'real' people who inhabit the country and their pragmatism gives me great hope for the survival of the 'real' China – although it won't be an easy task.

China now has a population of nearly 1.4 billion, which represents some 20 per cent of the world population (and means that approximately one person in five is Chinese). China is trying to feed that 20 per cent of world population with less than 10 per cent of the planet's arable land. But some 10 per cent of China's arable land – the land on which food grows – has been lost to development in the last ten years or so. As farmers move to the cities, either forced by expropriation of their land or lured by the promise of a better life, one wonders how the food supply can be maintained. If the cities are growing in size, and the farming land is diminishing, how on earth are the Chinese going to manage to feed themselves? They have always been clever about utilising the most unlikely space to produce food – I'm thinking of rice terraces snaking up hillsides, especially in Yunnan, the 'peri-urban' plots of greenery grown at city roadsides and in public gardens, fish in paddyfields, turtle ponds, aquaculture in general. However, with less land on which to produce the staples – rice in the south, wheat in the north – the traditional Chinese mode of eating may have to radically change.

In a sense it already has, with the influx of Western-type foods and food chains. Meat is now seen as a necessary part of the diet when, previously, it was a rare treat, more of a flavouring for vegetables. (Meat dishes in Western Chinese restaurants are uncharacteristic of real Chinese cooking.) Where and how will all the meat-producing animals be raised? Dairy farming has recently been encouraged by the government, although over 90 per cent of the adult population is lactose intolerant to a certain degree. Where and how will all the milk-producing animals be raised? As China gets richer, and with a burgeoning middle class, will women be happy to spend hours making wontons and dumplings, or will they start to buy them ready-made? And, most frighteningly, if young Chinese take to the hamburgers and pizzas now being introduced, will the next generation actually know how to cook their own traditional dishes?

However, in our travels around China, we encountered eaters, thinkers, cooks and producers and all were incredibly enthusiastic about what they were doing. They all intend to hold on to what they value from the past, but perhaps – rather like Ching and I – would probably choose to ally it with a hint of the new. Hong Kong, for instance, is the showcase for a balance between the old and traditional and the new and progressive, certainly in terms of food, so perhaps this is the way China will go. The Chinese have survived much worse, re-emerging from chaos, and I think they can do so again. I sincerely hope so.

It was wonderful being in China again, visiting familiar and unfamiliar places – and tasting some wonderful food. Travelling the length and breadth of the country with Ken and the film crew, I realised just how vast China is; it could swallow Europe, and some of its cities boast as many inhabitants as a single European country. Although there are shared threads, there really is no such thing as 'Chinese cuisine': the cooking styles of China's regions – influenced variously by geography, climate and history – are as different as those of countries in northern and southern Europe.

Food has such a central role in Chinese culture that, country-wide, one of the most common greetings translates as: 'Have you eaten yet?' I like that! Formally, there are eight distinctive regional cuisines (Shandong, Sichuan, Guangdong, Fujian, Jiangsu, Zhejiang, Hunan and Anhui). Many commentators, however, divide the country into gastronomic quarters: Beijing and the north, Shanghai and the east, Sichuan and the west, Guangzhou (Canton) and the south. But even these simpler divisions do not take into account further variations: Chinese Muslims and Buddhists have their individual styles of cooking, as do the minority ethnic groups – some 56 of them – that co-exist with the majority Han Chinese. But cooking and eating with the Dai minority and the Bulang tea-pickers was a delight for me in Yunnan, and experiencing Muslim food with the Uighurs in Kashgar, in the far north, was an eye-opener – as were the hats!

Whichever region they come from, Han Chinese all comply with the principle of balance denoted by yin and yang. In a culinary sense, yin means 'cool' and yang 'hot', and there are cooking techniques and ingredients that belong in each of the two camps. By cooking and eating in this balanced way, the Chinese believe an essential equilibrium is maintained, which ensures good health. Some restaurants cook with these principles in mind, and shops sell herbs that can be added to food. Some foods themselves are meant to be good for certain parts of the body: snake, for instance, is believed to be an aphrodisiac. Food as medicine wasn't a new concept to me, but I got valuable further insights through many of the people we talked to. And although they're said to be warming for the blood and good for the skin, I don't think I'll be eating fried scorpions any time soon – although Ken seemed to take a liking to them at a street-food stall in Wangfujing in Beijing...

Other shared threads of Chinese cooking are the balancing of the characteristics of a Chinese meal. Dishes should have fragrance, taste (sour, sweet, salty, bitter, piquant), shape, colour and mouth-feel: the latter subdivides into textural tenderness, crunchiness, crispiness, smoothness and softness (and explains why the Chinese have such a love for things like chicken feet). Another facet of Chinese eating is the love of snacks: from the *xiao chi* (small eats) of Sichuan to the *dim sum* of Hong Kong. Now, of course, with China having opened up to Western ideas and Western foods, some of these snacks might just be hamburgers, cheese or pizzas, which is worrying. The Chinese are already starting to suffer from Western health problems such as obesity, and if this continues, their historical reverence for food, its traditions and its role in Chinese culture might be eroding. This would be such a pity for, even though I am Taiwanese, I am full of admiration for my mainland neighbours – supposed 'opponents/adversaries' – for their fortitude, for their culinary creativity, and for the history that we share.

DUMPLINGS AND APPETISERS

CHENGDU WONTON

Growing up in a Cantonese household I was very familiar with wontons. I knew I was in for a treat when I first had them in Chengdu, but I was not prepared for the lake of chilli oil and spices they came in. Luckily, I have always liked spicy food. This recipe is for other such lovers of spicy food.

Serves 4 as a starter or 2 as a meal

50g (2oz) Chinese dried black mushrooms, pre-soaked in warm water
for about 20 minutes until soft and pliable
450g (1lb) minced fatty pork
4 tablespoons finely chopped Chinese chives (or spring onions)
1 egg white
2 teaspoons sesame oil
salt and freshly ground black pepper
20–25 wonton wrappers, 10 x 10cm (4 x 4in), thawed if frozen

For the sauce
1 tablespoon groundnut or vegetable oil
1 tablespoon chilli oil (see page 264)
1 tablespoon finely chopped garlic
2 tablespoons finely chopped spring onions
1 tablespoon roasted and ground Sichuan peppercorns
3 tablespoons sesame paste (or peanut butter)
2 tablespoons light soy sauce
1 tablespoon sugar
2 teaspoons chilli bean sauce
85ml (3fl oz) chicken stock

Squeeze the excess water out of the mushrooms, then cut off and discard the woody stems. Finely chop the mushrooms and combine them with the meat, chives (or spring onions), egg white, sesame oil and salt and pepper. Mix well.

Place about 1 rounded teaspoon of filling in the middle of each wonton wrapper. Gather the four sides of the wrapper up over the filling, allowing the wonton skin to fold in pleats naturally. Gently pinch the wrapper together at the top very well so it is sealed completely. Repeat this process until you have used up all the stuffing.

Heat a wok over high heat until it is hot, then add the groundnut or vegetable and chilli oils. Add the garlic and spring onions and stir-fry for 20 seconds, then add the rest of the ingredients and simmer for 5 minutes. Transfer the sauce to a separate bowl.

Bring a medium-sized pot of water to a boil and poach the dumplings for about 3 minutes, or until they float to the top. Remove and drain, then serve with the sauce.

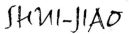

SHUI-JIAO
Pork and prawn chive water dumplings

Dumplings are a staple food found in the north of China, but various types are also found in many different regions – both steamed and pan-fried. My favourite are these *shui-jiao* dumplings, which are cooked in boiling water and then served with a soy vinegar dipping sauce. You can vary the filling ingredients, but this is my all-time favourite.

Serves 2–4

30 wheat flour dumpling skins
1 tablespoon groundnut oil

For the filling
150g (5oz) tiger prawns, peeled, deveined (see page 147) and minced
60g (2½oz) minced pork
3 tablespoons Chinese chives (garlic chives), finely chopped
4 whole tinned water chestnuts, finely diced
1 tablespoon oyster sauce
1 tablespoon Shaoxing rice wine (or dry sherry)
sea salt and freshly ground white pepper

For the dipping sauce
2 tablespoons light soy sauce
2 tablespoons Chinese clear (plain) rice vinegar (or cider vinegar)
2 teaspoons toasted sesame oil
a small handful of fresh coriander leaves, finely chopped

For the garnish
a small handful of finely chopped fresh coriander

Put all the ingredients for the filling into a bowl and, using one hand, knead and squeeze the filling through your fingers to combine all the flavours. Wash and dry your hands. Place a dumpling skin in the palm of your hand. Place a heaped teaspoon of filling in the middle of the dumpling skin, then dip your finger into water and brush around the edge of the skin. Fold the skin in half over the filling, pressing down on the edges to make sure they stick together well. Pleat the edges of the dumpling four times, pinching well to secure. (You could make the dumplings ahead to this point, then freeze in an airtight container and cook from frozen when you like.) Combine all the ingredients for the dipping sauce in a small bowl and put to one side.

Heat a pan of water (about 1 litre/1¾ pints) and bring to the boil. Add the groundnut oil and reduce the heat to medium, then add the dumplings and cook for 3–4 minutes until they float to the surface and are cooked through. Using a slotted spoon, scoop them out into dishes, garnish with chopped coriander and serve them immediately, with the dipping sauce.

CHINA   Dumplings and appetisers

SUI MAI DUMPLINGS

Dim sum is the southern Chinese ritual of drinking tea and eating sweet and savoury snacks of all sorts. Although some snacks exist elsewhere in China, it is the Cantonese who have elevated them to a true art. There are literally countless different types of *dim sum* snacks, depending on the chef and his or her interests. Steaming is a favourite technique of the Cantonese, cooking food gently so that subtle flavours are not masked by the ferocity of frying in hot oil, for example. These delectable *sui mai* dumplings are easy to make at home. They are perfect for the Cantonese, as ovens do not exist in most Chinese kitchens. These dumplings make a terrific beginning to any meal.

Serves 4–6

225g (8oz) wonton skins, thawed if frozen
fresh coriander leaves

For the filling
250g (9oz) raw tiger prawns, peeled, deveined (see page 147) and coarsely chopped
250g (9oz) minced fatty pork
1 teaspoon salt
½ teaspoon freshly ground white pepper
100g (4oz) fresh or tinned water chestnuts, peeled if fresh,
    drained if tinned, and finely minced
1½ tablespoons light soy sauce
2 tablespoons finely chopped spring onions
1 tablespoon Shaoxing rice wine (or dry sherry)
1 teaspoon sugar
2 teaspoons sesame oil
1 egg white, lightly beaten

To serve
dipping sauces of your choice

Put the prawns and pork into a large bowl or a food processor, add the salt and pepper and mix well, either by kneading with your hand, stirring with a wooden spoon, or pulsing. Then add all the other filling ingredients and stir them well into the prawn and pork mixture. Cover the bowl with clingfilm and chill for at least 20 minutes.

Place a portion of filling on to each wonton skin. Bring up the sides and press them around the filling mixture. Tap the dumpling on the bottom to make a flat base. The top should be wide open, exposing the meat filling. Now place a coriander leaf on top. Repeat this process until you have used up all the filling.

Place the dumplings in a bamboo steamer lined with damp cheesecloth. Place the steamer over water in a wok or pot, cover tightly and steam over high heat for 15 minutes. Serve immediately with dipping sauces of your choice.

SPRING ONION PANCAKES

You will find this savoury snack both in the restaurants in Beijing (Peking) and sold at the street food stalls of Kashgar. Contrary to what most people think, wheat is the main food here in northern China. These pancakes remind me of Middle Eastern snacks, perhaps the result of an exchange with Arab traders on the Silk Road? You have the option of making them as rolled onion cakes or flat, a bit like pizza. Either way, they are equally delicious. Be particularly careful when deep-frying in a wok.

Makes around 9 flat onion cakes or 18 rolled onion cakes

1 x recipe Chinese pancakes (see page 99)
2 eggs, beaten
9 spring onions, finely chopped
salt and freshly ground black pepper
900ml (1½ pints) groundnut or vegetable oil

If you are making the flat onion cakes, take two pancakes and brush one side of each with beaten egg, then sprinkle one with spring onions, salt and pepper. Press the other pancake, egg-brushed side down, on top to seal.

If you are rolling them, take one pancake, brush one side with beaten egg, then sprinkle with spring onions, salt and pepper. Roll the pancake into a cylinder.

Heat a wok over high heat until it is hot. Add the oil, and when it is hot, hold each cake, either flat or rolled, with tongs and deep-fry until crispy. Drain on kitchen paper. Continue frying until you have fried all the pancakes.

Cut the pancakes into bite-sized pieces and serve immediately.

PICKLED SICHUAN CARROTS, ER CAI, GARLIC CHIVES AND RED ONION

This simple yet delicious pickle is superior to anything I have ever tasted. It is called *shi chao cai* ('take a bath vegetable'), which is a term used to describe a quick technique for pickling vegetables, and means that it's so quick you can make this before you take a bath, leave it overnight and it will be ready to eat the next day. The vegetables still retain their crunch, original flavour and crispness. I had the wonderful pleasure of making this dish with the grandmother of our friend Jenny Gao, who accompanied us for parts of the trip, and it reminded me of my own grandmother. I felt so appreciative and blessed to learn this from a woman who has clearly lived through some harsh times in China. She told us that a relative had bred a lamb during the Cultural Revolution to send to her so that she could have some extra food and protein when she was pregnant with Jenny's father. An extraordinary woman.

Makes 1 x 500ml (17fl oz) jar

For the pickling liquid
450ml (¾ pint) good-quality water
50g (2oz) good-quality salt
a small handful of Chinese white rock sugar (or granulated sugar)
a small handful of red rock sugar
225ml (8fl oz) good-quality *bai jiou* (distilled white liquor)

For the pickling vegetables
2 whole carrots, washed and dried
a few pieces of *er cai* (baby root vegetables), or use tender broccoli stalks,
    not broccoli flowers
1 red onion, peeled and quartered
tender inner stems of a small bunch of Chinese garlic chives (or baby spring
    onions), sliced into 2cm (¾in) lengths

To serve
1 teaspoon Sichuan pepper oil (see page 264)
1 tablespoon chilli oil (see page 264)

Place the water, salt, rock sugars and *bai jiou* into a Chinese ceramic pickling urn (or a sterilised glass jar). Mix well with chopsticks and stir well to dissolve. Add all the pickling vegetables and push down to submerge them well in the liquid. Place the lid on to seal the pickling urn. The pickling urn is surrounded by a small 'moat' – allowing you to fill the edges of the pickling urn lid with water to seal the urn, so that no air can seep in. Pickle overnight or for 1–2 days. To serve, slice the vegetables into bite-sized pieces. Season with the Sichuan pepper oil and the chilli oil.

PICKLED CUCUMBER with chilli

My obsession with pickles started when my mother used to send me off to school with a packed lunch of cold rice, pickles and stir-fried meat and vegetables. The pickles add a salty-sour flavour that is very *xia fan* – 'gives flavour to rice and helps make plain rice more palatable'. My favourite vegetable to pickle is cucumber and this delicious recipe pairs it with garlic, chilli bean paste, rice vinegar and chilli. This is a quick pickling technique, and the pickle should be eaten within a few days while the cucumbers still retain their crunch and freshness.

Serves 2–4

4 small cucumbers, sliced in half lengthways and de-seeded, each half cut into long wedge shapes and then sliced into 1cm (½in) pieces

For the marinade
1 garlic clove, peeled and minced
2 pinches of caster sugar
1 tablespoon Chinese clear (plain) rice vinegar (or cider vinegar)
1 teaspoon chilli bean paste
1 teaspoon chilli oil (see page 264)
1 tablespoon toasted sesame oil

For the garnish
1 fresh red chilli, de-seeded and cut into small strips

Combine all the ingredients for the marinade in a bowl. Add the cucumbers and leave to marinate in the fridge for 20 minutes.

Divide the mixture between small bowls, garnish with the fresh chilli and serve with plain rice and stir-fried vegetables for a light but flavourful dinner.

You can also make a batch of pickled cucumber and decant into sterilised glass jars, then keep refrigerated for up to 1 week. Spoon some into a chicken or vegetable stir-fry to add flavour.

GINGER AND SOY
CHILLI-STEAMED SCALLOPS

This is one of my go-to recipes for easy entertaining. Fresh scallops are such a treat and this makes a tasty appetiser or a shared main with other dishes. I like to make a simple seasoning liquid to dress the scallops, so that as they steam all the flavours are infused. Then a simple garnish of crispy garlic and shallots adds texture and fragrance to the final dish. Enjoy!

Serves 4 as a starter

4 large king scallops in their shells
50ml (2fl oz) groundnut oil
2 medium shallots, peeled and finely chopped
6 large garlic cloves, peeled and finely chopped

For the seasoning sauce
1 fresh medium red chilli, de-seeded and chopped
2.5cm (1in) piece fresh root ginger, peeled and grated
1 teaspoon toasted sesame oil
1 tablespoon groundnut oil
1 garlic clove, peeled and finely chopped
1 tablespoon light soy sauce

For the garnish
fresh coriander leaves

Using a sharp knife, carefully prise open the scallop shells by running the knife on the inside of the shell to release the membrane attached to it. (Or ask your fishmonger to prepare the scallops for you.) I like to leave the bright orange coral attached, but you can discard it if you like. Wash the scallops in cold running water.

Combine all the ingredients for the seasoning sauce in a small bowl and put to one side.

Place the scallops on a heatproof plate that fits inside a bamboo steamer and spoon 1 teaspoon of the sauce over each one. Put the plate into the steamer. Half-fill the wok with boiling water, place the steamer over the wok (making sure the base doesn't touch the water), then cover and steam the scallops for 5–6 minutes.

Meanwhile, heat a wok over high heat, then add the groundnut oil. Fry the shallots and garlic until crisp (it should take less than 1 minute). Pour the oil through a sieve into a heatproof bowl and drain the shallots and garlic on kitchen paper.

Serve the scallops sprinkled with the crispy shallots and garlic and garnished with coriander.

GUANGDONG

GUANGDONG and Cantonese cooking

The province of Guangdong, in the south of China, has a particular resonance for me, because it is where my mother's family come from: she was brought up in Kaiping (Hoiping), a small town in the region, and I have relatives there still. Before she died, my mother and I made a pilgrimage back from Chicago to Kaiping to meet the remnants of our family. The filming of this series has happily allowed me to return yet again to see them, to re-explore the delights of Cantonese cuisine, and to pay homage to my ancestors.

Guangdong lies on the South China Sea, and its capital is Guangzhou, which is known historically as Canton. This word is believed to have originated from the Portuguese name for Guangzhou, 'Cantão', and of course this is where the name of the cuisine, Cantonese, comes from. Guangzhou, one of the largest cities in China, has been a nationally important river trading port for thousands of years. From the 17th century it was one of only four Chinese cities allowed to trade with foreigners (and through which, shamefully, much British opium came). Guangzhou may have a long history, but another Guangdong city, Shenzhen, further to the east, is known for its lack of history. In some thirty years, the sleepy fishing village of Shenzhen has transformed itself into a modern metropolis, its population swelling from thousands to many millions. And in fact, the whole of Guangdong, because of its geography and the vivacity and adaptability of its people, has played a huge part in what is known as the 'Chinese revival'.

The cooking style of the area is, naturally, Cantonese. Many people regard Cantonese as the haute cuisine of China – possibly due to the influence of chefs of the Imperial Court who fled to Guangzhou in the 17th century – and the city is still rightly called the gastronomic capital of China. (There is a local saying: 'every five steps a restaurant', which is almost true!) Cantonese is the style of cooking I grew up with – my mother introduced me to its tastes and flavours in our home in Chicago – and it is still my favourite Chinese cuisine (though closely followed by Sichuan). It is also probably the most familiar of Chinese cooking styles throughout the rest of the world, for the majority of Chinese nationals opening restaurants and cooking in other countries come from Guangdong and Hong Kong.

The essence of Cantonese cooking, one of the eight major styles of Chinese cuisine, is its freshness: many restaurants in the area have water tanks filled with seafood, and cages of fowl and other creatures, waiting for you to choose. Cooking techniques are straightforward – boiling, steaming and stir-frying using little oil – so that the purity of the fresh ingredient can be truly appreciated. Flavouring condiments, of which there are many, are used reservedly – a dash here and there only, to complement the dish's

principal ingredient – and often are served at the table, for diners to help themselves. Spices are used sparingly – star anise, garlic and chilli among them – and herbs rarely. Oyster sauce, for instance, one of the key ingredients of Cantonese cooking, is said to have been invented in Guangdong in the 1800s. Fish and chicken particularly benefit from this careful cooking and flavouring: prawns are marinated in liquor, to make them 'drunk' (literally, for sometimes they are still alive), then simply flamed or boiled; fish is steamed with minimal flavours (spring onion, ginger, soy); and although chicken can be steamed too, it is also cooked in the Cantonese style (basted, dried, then fried). Pork, the favourite meat of most of China, is treated somewhat differently: it can be marinated and barbecued, roasted, stir-fried, served with a sauce or minced for a dumpling filling.

Vegetables play a large part in all the Chinese cuisines, and Cantonese is no exception. Most are squeaky fresh – just plucked from the ground, such as those I enjoyed when I visited my relations in Kaiping – but many are preserved in some way. (In Guangdong, this may come from the Hakka people, a subdivision of the Han Chinese, found mostly in Guangdong and Taiwan.) Most cultures dry or preserve foods for times of hardship or simply for the winter, and the textures of some dried, salted or pickled vegetables, and indeed fish and meats, in Cantonese cooking, is a key pleasure when tasting many of the dishes. Another preservation method employs fermentation, and fermented dofu (tofu), black beans and other pulses contribute amazing flavour (soy sauce is made from fermented soya beans). And of course, rice is the staple of the Cantonese diet; the province is known as one of the 'rice-bowls' of China.

Another aspect of Cantonese food is its snacks. The Chinese as a nation are great snackers and love eating on the hoof and on the street, but nowhere more so than in Guangdong and Hong Kong (for *dim sum*, see page 55). Dumplings and wontons, noodles and buns – made with rice, wheat, rye, barley, sorghum or millet flour – are on offer from street-food stalls everywhere, with a never-ending variety of fillings. Noodles of all kinds – *jook sing* are made with duck eggs and are traditionally rolled by a chef sitting on a length of bamboo log! – are served in savoury broths. Often on offer is a long-cooked soup, *lou fo tong* ('old fire-cooked soup') containing medicinal herbs the Cantonese believe will heal and strengthen. Another snack occasionally seen is 'deep-fried milk' – unusual in a culture that traditionally does not eat dairy products (most Chinese are actually lactose intolerant); I have encountered it several times and it's good. Many street stalls also sell little custard tarts – you can try my version of these treats on page 254.

It is snacks like these that are given as ritual offerings to our ancestors. Ancestor worship lies at the heart of religion in China: those who remain take care of the deceased as if they were still alive. Gifts include food, drink, money and favourite goods – such as cars, washing machines, mobile phones – which are all made of cardboard and paper (and bought from special mourning shops). These are burned, so that the smoke carries the messages upwards to the heavens. I was lucky enough to be in China at the right time for *Qing Ming*, the traditional tomb-sweeping ceremony, and I was able therefore to pay my respects to my forebears.

SOUPS AND SALADS

SEA BASS, BABY PAK CHOY
and coriander soup

This is a clean-tasting and nourishing soup. Fresh sea bass, shiitake mushrooms and baby pak choy are gently poached in a simple vegetable broth and then garnished with fresh, aromatic coriander. The result is a sweet, healthy soup that is perfect as a starter or a light supper.

Serves 2 as a main and 4 as a starter

250g (9oz) sea bass fillets, skin on, each fillet
    cut into 4 strips
800ml (1 pint 8fl oz) water
2.5cm (1in) piece fresh root ginger, grated
1 tablespoon Shaoxing rice wine (or dry sherry)
3 fresh shiitake mushrooms, sliced
4 small baby pak choy, sliced in half
    down the middle
1 tablespoon vegetable bouillon stock powder
a dash of toasted sesame oil
sea salt and freshly ground white pepper
a small handful of fresh coriander

Rinse the fish in cold running water.

Pour the water into a pan or wok and bring to the boil. Add the fish and all the ingredients up to and including the bouillon stock powder. Turn the heat to medium and cook for 5 minutes. Season with the sesame oil and salt and white pepper to taste. Stir in the coriander, transfer to serving bowls and serve immediately.

XI SHI DOFU SOUP

Often for the Chinese, a soup can be a hearty one-dish meal. In this case, the soup contains meat, prawns and vegetables as well as dofu (tofu). The dofu absorbs the rich flavours of the broth and makes a comforting, satisfying main course with rice on a wintry evening.

Serves 4

50g (2oz) Chinese dried black mushrooms, pre-soaked in warm water
    for about 20 minutes until soft and pliable, then drained
1½ tablespoons groundnut or vegetable oil
1 tablespoon finely chopped fresh ginger
225g (8oz) pork spareribs, separated into individual ribs
3 tablespoons Shaoxing rice wine (or dry sherry)
1 teaspoon sugar
salt and freshly ground white pepper
1.2 litres (2 pints) chicken stock
450g (1lb) fresh silken or soft dofu (tofu)
100g (4oz) raw tiger prawns, peeled, deveined (see page 147)
    and cut into 2.5cm (1in) pieces
4 tablespoons finely chopped spring onions
2 teaspoons sesame oil

Rinse the mushrooms well and squeeze out any excess liquid. Discard the tough stems, then shred the caps and put them aside.

Heat the wok until it is very hot, then add the oil. When the oil is hot, add the ginger, then the spareribs and stir-fry for about 5 minutes, then add the rice wine (or sherry), sugar, salt, pepper and stock. Add the mushrooms and bring to a boil, then lower the heat, cover and simmer for 15 minutes.

Meanwhile, gently cut the dofu into 2.5cm (1in) cubes and drain on kitchen paper.

Carefully add the cubed dofu and the prawn pieces to the soup and simmer, uncovered, for another 3 minutes. Finally, add the spring onions, adjust the seasoning with salt and pepper, drizzle with the sesame oil and serve.

MAK'S WONTON NOODLE SOUP

In London it is not uncommon to see Rolls-Royces parked in front of fish and chip shops because no matter how successful someone becomes, they can still yearn for good comfort food. In Hong Kong, a good equivalent would be Mak's Noodles Ltd, an extremely modest classic restaurant that serves some of the best wonton noodle soup in all of Hong Kong. It is a great soup, with juicy dumplings – pure simplicity, brilliantly executed – supreme comfort food for every Cantonese diner.

Serves 4–6

100g (4oz) wonton skins
1.2 litres (2 pints) chicken stock
1 tablespoon light soy sauce
1 teaspoon sesame oil
175g (6oz) thin fresh or dried Chinese egg noodles

Filling for the wontons
100g (4oz) peeled, uncooked prawns, deveined (see page 147) and coarsely chopped
100g (4oz) minced pork
salt and freshly ground white pepper
1 tablespoon light soy sauce
2 tablespoons finely chopped spring onions
1 tablespoon Shaoxing rice wine (or dry sherry)
1 teaspoon sugar
1 teaspoon sesame oil
½ egg white, lightly beaten

For the garnish
chopped spring onions

To make the filling, put the prawns and pork into a large bowl, add salt and pepper and mix well, either by kneading with your hand or by stirring with a wooden spoon. Then add all the other filling ingredients and stir them well into the prawn and pork mixture. Cover the bowl with clingfilm and chill for at least 20 minutes.

When you are ready to stuff the wontons, put 1 tablespoon of the filling in the centre of the first wonton skin. Dampen the edges with a little water and bring up the sides of the skin around the filling. Pinch the edges together at the top so that the wonton is sealed – it should look like a small filled bag. Repeat with the remaining wonton skins and filling.

When the wontons are ready, bring the stock, soy sauce and sesame oil to a simmer in a large pot.

In another large pot, bring lightly salted water to a boil and poach the wontons for 1 minute or until they float to the surface. Remove them immediately and transfer to the pot with the stock. Blanch the noodles in the salted water for 1 minute, then drain and add to the pot with the stock and dumplings. This procedure will result in a cleaner tasting broth. Continue to simmer the wontons and noodles in the stock for 2 minutes. Transfer to either a large soup bowl or to individual bowls, garnish with spring onions and serve at once.

DAI AUNTY RIVER FISH SOUP

The Dai people are an ethnic minority who live in the southwest of China (see pages 130–133). I had the honour of cooking with a Dai 'aunty', who took me fishing in a nearby stream, and then we cooked together with her family in her modest wooden home. The women in the village are responsible for cooking and looking after the children. They use small nets to catch the river fish, but also find in their nets water millipede, baby freshwater shrimp and baby freshwater crabs. Dai Aunty would expertly prepare all these ingredients – gutting each fish with one fast swoop of a small knife, removing the 'dead man's fingers' (the lungs) from the crabs – and then cook them in a delicious spicy, sour broth. These Dai women were an inspiration – they may not possess material wealth, but they have soul.

Serves 4–6 to share

750ml (1 pint 7fl oz) water

200g (7oz) tender baby bamboo shoots (or tinned bamboo shoots, drained and rinsed)

6 small fresh chillies, sliced

2.5cm (1in) piece fresh root ginger, peeled and finely chopped

1 small bunch of Vietnamese mint (or a few stalks of fresh lemon grass, peeled, bruised and cut into 5cm/2in pieces), roughly chopped

½ teaspoon salt

300g (11oz) mix of small river fish, shrimp, crabs (or mixed seafood medley of shrimp, mussels and scallops), cleaned and rinsed

a small handful of freshly chopped wild coriander (or farmed coriander)

Bring the water to the boil in a medium pot. Add the bamboo shoots, chillies, ginger and mint (or lemon grass). Once the water has come back to the boil, add the salt, then the seafood and cook for 3 minutes on medium heat. Take off the heat, add the chopped coriander and serve immediately.

PEKING DUCK SOUP

Beijing's top duck restaurants not only offer Peking duck, but also an entire duck extravaganza that features every imaginable part of the duck except the quack. These may include delectable offerings such as duck's tongue with mustard sauce, duck gizzard stir-fried with vegetables or duck liver with spicy sauce. Duck entrails as well as duck feet, often braised, are considered delicacies. The feast often finishes with a soup made using the bones of the roast duck as the base. It is a savoury and refreshing end for any true lover of duck.

Serves 4

carcass of roasted Peking duck (see pages 230–233 or 234–237)
50g (2oz) preserved mustard greens, soaked in several changes of cold water
1.2 litres (2 pints) chicken stock
salt and freshly ground black pepper
1 teaspoon sugar
2 teaspoons Shaoxing rice wine (or dry sherry)

Rinse the cavity of the duck to rid it of the spices. Chop the carcass into large pieces.

Drain the mustard greens thoroughly and chop coarsely.

Bring the stock to the boil in a large pot. Add the duck bones and simmer for 20 minutes. Remove the bones with a strainer, skim the stock, then add the mustard greens, salt, pepper, sugar and rice wine (or sherry) and continue to simmer, uncovered, for 10 minutes. Serve the soup immediately in individual bowls or in a large soup tureen.

VEGETARIAN HOT AND SOUR SOUP

I never tire of a good hot and sour soup. The trick is the fine balance of sour to spicy without making it unpalatable. This dish should have lots of flavour, while the crunchy bamboo shoots, wood ear mushrooms, preserved Sichuan vegetables and fresh dofu (tofu) all add layers of *kou-gan* (texture), which is so important in Chinese cooking. This is a satisfying soup for any time of the year. Meat lovers can add cooked chicken or Chinese roast pork pieces.

Serves 4

1 litre (1¾ pints) vegetable stock
1 tablespoon freshly grated root ginger
2 fresh red chillies, de-seeded and finely chopped
1 tablespoon Shaoxing rice wine (or dry sherry)
2 tablespoons dark soy sauce
1 x 220g tin bamboo shoots, drained
10g (¼oz) Chinese dried wood ear mushrooms,
   pre-soaked in hot water for 20 minutes, then drained
250g (9oz) fresh firm dofu (tofu), cut into cubes
50g (2oz) Sichuan preserved vegetables, rinsed and sliced
2 tablespoons light soy sauce
3 tablespoons Chinese black rice vinegar (or balsamic vinegar)
1 tablespoon chilli oil (see page 264)
a pinch of freshly ground white pepper
1 egg, lightly beaten
1 tablespoon cornflour, blended with 2 tablespoons cold water
1 large spring onion, finely sliced

For the garnish (optional)
fresh coriander leaves

Pour the stock into a pan and bring to the boil. Add all the ingredients up to and including the wood ear mushrooms and cook for 1 minute. Turn the heat down to medium, add the dofu, Sichuan vegetables, soy sauce, vinegar, chilli oil and white pepper, then simmer for 10 minutes.

Stir in the egg, then add the blended cornflour and stir to thicken the soup (add more if you like a thicker consistency).

Add the spring onion, garnish with the coriander, if you like, and serve immediately.

YI JIN'S DAI-INSPIRED RICE NOODLE SOUP

This delightful recipe was inspired by Yi Jin, who with her young husband, Ai Han En Loug, makes 350kg (772lb) of fresh rice noodles every day at their home in Yunnan. Produced in a home-made artisanal factory in their garage, the noodles are quite sought after in Jinghong. The secret is the amount of water they use with the rice flour. The result is a slightly chewy rice noodle that is equally good stir-fried or used in this soup, which they made especially for me. It was a simple but comforting, savoury and satisfying dish.

Serves 2–4

225g (8oz) round, dried rice noodles, soaked in warm water for 25 minutes, then drained
1½ tablespoons groundnut or vegetable oil
2 tablespoons coarsely chopped garlic
2 tablespoons coarsely chopped fresh ginger
2 teaspoons dried red chilli flakes
100g (4oz) minced pork
salt and freshly ground black pepper
100g (4oz) fresh tomatoes, cut into quarters
1.2 litres (2 pints) hot chicken stock
1½ tablespoons light soy sauce
2 teaspoons Shaoxing rice wine (or dry sherry)
3 tablespoons finely chopped spring onions

Blanch the drained rice noodles in salted boiling water for 5 minutes. Drain thoroughly, then set aside until you are ready to use them.

Heat a wok or large frying pan over high heat until it is hot. Add the oil, and when it is very hot and slightly smoking, add the garlic, ginger and chilli flakes and stir-fry for 30 seconds. Add the pork, salt and pepper and continue to stir-fry for 3 minutes. Now stir in the tomatoes. Finally, add the stock, soy sauce and rice wine (or sherry) and turn the heat to low, then cover and simmer for 5 minutes. Skim off any surface fat, then add the noodles and cook for another 3–4 minutes.

Stir in the spring onions and continue to simmer for 2 minutes. Ladle into a large soup tureen and serve at once.

FRESH SOY SUGAR TOMATO SALAD

While in Cuandixia, a village a couple of hours away from Beijing, I met Mrs Han, one of the locals. She prepared some large, ripe beef tomatoes by quartering them and then sprinkling sugar over them. I suggested adding some light soy sauce. The result is a delicious, savoury-sweet tomato salad.

Serves 2–4

2 large, ripe beef tomatoes, quartered and halved again, stalks and seeds discarded
1 teaspoon granulated sugar
2 tablespoons light soy sauce

Place the tomato slices in the fridge for at least 15 minutes before assembling.

Place the chilled tomatoes on a plate and sprinkle with the sugar, then drizzle the light soy sauce over them. Stir together at the table and serve immediately.

DA DONG-INSPIRED PEKING DUCK SALAD

Da Dong is an inspirational Beijing chef. He is famed for his Peking Duck, a version which is healthier as it has less fat than usual. Over thirty years he has perfected his technique of roasting the Peking duck in a slow, fruit-wood-fired oven for double the amount of time that it usually takes, thus cooking out all the fat from beneath the skin. It was a delight to be able to use his Peking duck in a delicious duck salad and this is a great dish to make if you have any leftover roast duck pieces. Seasoning it with Chinese five-spice, dusting with cornflour and then deep-frying elevates the flavour of the duck, giving it another crispy edge. I was worried that the dish would not work because of the smaller amounts of fat in Da Dong's duck – that it would make my dish too dry – but it worked like a dream. He thought the dish was clever and delicious, which is a great compliment coming from such an ingenious chef! I served the duck with some garnishes borrowed from Da Dong, but I also made a delicious sauce-like dressing using wheat flour bean paste (*tian mian jiang*), sugar, black rice vinegar and XO sauce (a rich chilli sauce-oil containing dried shrimp, scallops and Jinhua ham, a dry-cured ham). You can substitute yellow bean paste mixed with Hoisin sauce for the *tian mian jiang* and you can buy the XO sauce from a Chinese supermarket, or mix a good chilli sauce with chilli oil.

Serves 2–4 to share

- 1 Granny Smith apple, unpeeled, halved, cored and sliced into thin half-moon shapes
- 1 Chinese pear, halved and sliced into thin half-moon shapes
- 1 large red radish, sliced lengthways into julienne strips
- 1 spring onion, sliced lengthways into julienne strips
- 1 tablespoon Sichuan pickle or grated red radish mixed with a splash of rice vinegar
- 500ml (17fl oz) vegetable oil
- 250g (9oz) Peking roast duck (see pages 230–233 or 234–237), boned and cut into small pieces
- ¼ teaspoon Chinese five-spice powder
- 2 tablespoons cornflour

For the dressing
- 3 tablespoons wheat flour bean paste (*tian mian jiang*, or 1 part yellow bean paste mixed with 4 parts Hoisin sauce)
- 1 tablespoon granulated sugar
- 2 tablespoons Chinese black rice vinegar (or balsamic vinegar)
- 1 tablespoon XO sauce (½ tablespoon each chilli sauce and chilli oil, see page 264)

For the garnish
a small handful of micro herbs
a small handful of edible yellow flowers
2 pastry birds for decoration (optional)

Place the apple and pear slices down the centre of a large, long, rectangular serving plate, to make heart shapes. Place some red radish strips down the middle of the hearts, then top with spring onion strips. Decorate the rest of the plate with sprinkles of Sichuan pickle.

Pour the oil into a wok and heat to 180°C/350°F, or until a cube of bread turns golden brown in 15 seconds. Dust the duck pieces with Chinese five-spice and then with the cornflour. Lower the pieces into the hot oil and deep-fry until crispy and the edges of the cornflour have turned golden brown. Lift out and drain on kitchen paper. Place the duck down the middle of the apple, pear, radish and spring onion strips on the serving plate.

Mix together all the dressing ingredients in a small bowl. Spoon some of this dressing over the duck pieces. Garnish the duck with micro herbs and decorate the plate with some edible yellow flowers (and I also added pastry birds borrowed from Da Dong).

LOTUS ROOT SALAD

The Chinese have shown great ingenuity over the centuries, turning the most unlikely vegetables into delectable dishes. The lotus is revered in China for its flower, leaves and root. The pattern of the root when sliced makes a stunning visual treat and the crunchy texture turns it into a delightful salad. A good friend from Beijing shared her recipe for this quick and unusual salad. I am forever grateful.

Serves 4

225g (8oz) fresh lotus root
2 teaspoons finely chopped fresh ginger
6 spring onions, finely chopped
3 tablespoons Chinese clear (plain) rice vinegar (or cider vinegar)
salt and freshly ground black pepper
2 teaspoons sugar

Wash the lotus root well in cold running water, then peel and slice it thinly crossways. Put it into a large bowl with all the remaining ingredients and toss gently. Leave for 15 minutes, then serve at once.

KASHGAR-INSPIRED SALAD

Uighur cuisine and culture was quite alien to me, as was the use of mutton in steamed dumplings, noodles (*laghman*) and samsa (baked dumplings) – I'm not a huge fan of mutton since it has such a strong flavour.

Ken and I were invited to a spring festival New Year party. Ken made a saffron vegetable rice and I made this colourful salad using the best of their local produce. I was particularly in love with the yellow 'carrot' or 'radish' – it was sweeter and less hardy than the orange carrot. The men and women were separated at the party, which I thought was rather 'un-festive', but that is the Muslim tradition – in Chinese culture you eat together with your family at New Year. However, the women all seemed to enjoy the salad that I made, with the female head of the family helping herself to seconds!

Serves 2–4 to share

- 1 carrot, peeled and sliced into long, thin julienne strips
- 1 yellow carrot (or yellow pepper, de-seeded), peeled and sliced into long, thin julienne strips
- 1 large fresh green chilli, de-seeded and thinly sliced
- 1 large bunch of Chinese celery (thin stalk variety), leaves and stalks finely chopped
- 1 small bunch of fresh coriander, finely chopped
- a small handful of green raisins, finely chopped
- a small handful of apricot kernels, finely chopped (you can buy these in health food shops)
- 2 large ripe pomegranates, halved and seeds removed by hitting the sides using a wooden spoon and collecting the seeds in a bowl
- 3–4 tablespoons Chinese black rice vinegar (or balsamic vinegar)
- 3 tablespoons chilli oil (see page 264)
- 2 small pinches of salt

For the garnish
2 teaspoons raw (untoasted) sesame seeds

Toss all the ingredients together in a bowl. Spoon onto a serving plate and garnish with sesame seeds.

HONG KONG

KEN'S HONG KONG: my second home

Hong Kong is a city that is always in motion. Every time I return, I marvel at the energy, the unrelenting pace of life, the vibrancy of the place. It is a hybrid city, being both east and west at the same time, and it is a city very close to my heart – and even closer to my stomach…

The 'original' Hong Kong – meaning 'fragrant harbour' – was an island off the south coast of Guangdong, and passed into British hands in 1842 because of tea and opium. In 19th-century Britain, the insatiable appetite for tea from China meant that Britain's gold and silver reserves were being used up: the solution was to 'pay' for the tea with opium grown in India. China, not surprisingly, did not want such an import, and so the two countries went to war. When China was defeated in the First Opium War, the British demanded and got the strategically placed Hong Kong island.

After winning the Second Opium War in 1860, Britain was ceded Kowloon, an area on the Chinese mainland opposite the island. Finally, in 1898, another convention extorted from an increasingly weakened China was the so-called New Territories, an area adjacent to Kowloon, and this was leased to Britain for 99 years. In the intervening years, it became obvious that more than the New Territories would have to be handed back, and in late 1984 an agreement was reached: China would take over the entire British Crown Colony in July 1997, but Hong Kong's unique free-enterprise economy would be maintained for at least 50 years.

You may wonder how a communist China could allow capitalist Hong Kong to exist as it is. In my opinion, the answer is simple – the Chinese also like being rich. Much of the investment flowing into Hong Kong in the 1990s was from China, and it still is today. China may be changing, and changing fast, but I think Hong Kong will continue to be China's window on the world as well as the service centre for the rest of the country. With its strong financial markets and business skills, Hong Kong is indispensable to China's fast-growing economy.

Hong Kong is also indispensable because of its cuisine, to me probably the world's finest. The basis of Hong Kong Cantonese cooking is deeply rooted in the rich and ancient traditions of the grand Chinese food culture. Canton may be the capital of Guangdong, but Hong Kong, since the 1950s, has become the place where you can enjoy the very best Chinese food (Cantonese, Shanghai, Fujian and Beijing, as well as European). There are thousands of restaurants, from the smallest street-food stalls to the most luxurious of hotel dining rooms, but all share the same passion: food in all its aspects is central to Hong Kong life (along with work, gambling and shopping).

KEN on Hong Kong

Cantonese is one of the major regional Chinese cuisines, and is described in more detail on pages 26–29. It is probably the most versatile of the cuisines because it has access to the widest range of ingredients. Hong Kong, because it is open to the world, has access to even more ingredients and ideas than elsewhere in Guangdong, and what is most interesting to me is how Hong Kong is assimilating new foods, ingredients and styles of cooking, and experimenting with them, transforming them into a new style. There is a glorious continuity and unity to Chinese cuisine, but there is also a willingness to adapt, to accept diversity, especially in Hong Kong. New techniques include coating meats in a marinade or light froth of egg white (called 'velveting'), making batters with yeast or baking powder, which are lighter and less oily, and using vegetable oil instead of lard.

No foodie visit to Hong Kong would be complete without trying some seafood dishes (prawns, crabs, oysters, river fish), some wonton soups, some noodles, barbecue pork and perhaps a Hakka speciality or two. You must try to eat at least one Chiu Chow meal, a popular regional southern style of cooking from around the Swatow district of eastern Guangdong province. The last time I ate Chiu Chow I insisted on an old favourite – steamed chicken feet with black bean sauce, which everyone else at the table politely declined. They did, however, join me to eat soy goose, another speciality of the cooking style: the bird is slowly braised in a rich broth of herbs and spices so it comes out very tender and savoury. Or you could try something even more exotic. You'll find bird's nest soup here (very tasty, although the idea puts many people off) – and sea cucumber. Both these special-occasion dishes are, quite justifiably, not cheap. Or you could venture even further into exotica: the Cantonese will eat anything, including snake, civet cat, barking deer or water turtle, the latter farmed in ponds everywhere in China. I have enjoyed roasted rice birds, small birds that fly down to feed on the rice paddies: they include finches and buntings. Or even rice worms, which are netted when the rice paddies flood: steamed, they are much appreciated by the Cantonese.

But the mode of eating that is most characteristic of Hong Kong is *dim sum*. The words mean 'heart's delight' or 'to touch the heart', and *dim sum* certainly touch mine. Whether poached, steamed, shallow- or deep-fried, the sheer variety of *dim sum* is staggering. I love sitting in a *dim sum* restaurant watching the waiters wheeling their carts around the tables, each cart piled high with bamboo baskets. You can choose from a variety of dumplings, stuffed with meat, vegetables, shellfish, wrapped in rice or wheat-dough casings; you can have spring rolls, fried taro, steamed spareribs, meat balls, pork buns, even some dessert *dim sum*. Because the portions are small, you can taste a great variety before you are full, something I love doing. And, of course, you must drink tea. In Cantonese, having *dim sum* is known as *yum cha*, which means 'drink tea meal'.

Neither wholly Eastern nor entirely Western, Hong Kong is *sui generis* – a phenomenon never seen previously and never likely to be duplicated. As someone once said, 'If Hong Kong didn't exist, it would have had to have been invented.' I, for one, am very glad that it was invented, as I love it.

RICE AND NOODLES

CONGEE WITH CENTURY EGGS
or salted duck eggs

You will find this satisfying, comforting food throughout southern China. It is akin to porridge in the West. I love it for breakfast, often accompanied by a fried doughnut. Century eggs are also known as preserved eggs, hundred-year eggs, thousand-year eggs and thousand-year-old eggs, and are made by preserving duck eggs in a mixture of clay, ash and salt, among other things, for anything up to several months. The resulting texture, flavour and smell is not to everyone's taste, but I have many non-Chinese friends who have become quite addicted to these eggs.

For the more timid, I would suggest salted duck eggs. These are made by soaking duck eggs in brine for a week or so. This results in thick liquid egg white and a firm-textured, round yolk that is bright orange-red in colour. It has a deliciously rich taste. If you are interested in sampling a really exotic taste of China, then this is a recipe for you.

Serves 4

4 century eggs (or 4 salted duck eggs, see above)
2 litres (3 pints) water
short grain or long grain rice measured to the 150ml (¼ pint) level
    in a measuring jug, unwashed
2 teaspoons salt
3 tablespoons finely chopped spring onions
2 tablespoons finely chopped fresh coriander

If you are using century eggs, simply rinse the shells and peel them, then cut them into quarters. If you are using salted duck eggs, crack the eggs into a small bowl.

Bring the water to the boil in a large pot and add the rice and salt. Let the mixture come back to the boil and give it several good stirs, then turn the heat down to low and cover the pot. Let the mixture simmer for about 1 hour, stirring occasionally.

Add the eggs and simmer, uncovered, for a further 10 minutes.

Just before serving, add the spring onions and coriander and serve at once. (If you like, congee can be made in advance. In which case, reheat it slowly and simply add some more water if the porridge is too thick.)

CHING'S LONGEVITY NOODLES
with garlic, sesame oil, salt and soy sauce

This is a very traditional dish served and eaten on special occasions such as Chinese New Year and, in particular, birthdays. The dish would typically be made for someone to wish them a long life. Noodle makers have to be very skilled to produce very fine noodles without breaking them and it is much harder than making thick udon noodles.

In Beijing, Ken and I requested some noodle chefs make thin *mian-sien* noodles and they made a bowl quicker than it takes to cook a packet of instant noodles! (You can buy packets of dried, thin, longevity wheat flour noodles. All you need to do is cook them in boiling water for less than 2 minutes and toss sesame oil through them to prevent them from sticking.)

I dressed the noodles they made with the ingredients with which we would traditionally serve the dish – garlic, salt, light soy and toasted sesame oil. Simple, but comforting, a reminder of home.

Serves 2 to share

500g (1lb 2oz) cooked thin wheat flour noodles (225g/8oz dried weight)
1 tablespoon minced garlic
1 tablespoon light soy sauce
2 tablespoons toasted sesame oil
a pinch of salt

Toss the noodles with the garlic, soy sauce and sesame oil. Season with a pinch of salt and mix well, without breaking the noodles. Eat immediately.

JI SHI LIANG MEIN Chicken noodle salad

Liang mein (Mandarin Chinese for 'cool noodle') is a popular snack eaten all over China and Taiwan. Different variations can be found all over Southeast Asia.

This recipe takes me back to my childhood, when my grandmother used to make this delicious, simple dish, especially in the hot summer months and she would make it differently every time. The salad can be varied according to your taste by changing the topping, dressing, proteins and noodles. This is not only super quick to make, but also super healthy.

Serves 2 or 4 to share

200g (7oz) dried or fresh Chinese egg noodles
toasted sesame oil
100g (4oz) cucumber, de-seeded and shredded using a mandolin
100g (4oz) carrot, peeled and shredded using a mandolin
300g (11oz) cooked and shredded chicken

For the dressing
2 tablespoons light soy sauce
2 tablespoons Chinese clear (plain) rice vinegar (or cider vinegar)
1 tablespoon toasted sesame oil
1 teaspoon minced garlic
50g (2oz) smooth peanut butter
1 tablespoon water
juice of ½ lemon

To serve
a small handful of finely chopped fresh coriander
a pinch of hot chilli powder

Cook the noodles according to the instructions on the packet, then drain and refresh under cold running water. Drizzle with sesame oil and mix well to prevent them from sticking together, then place in a large bowl. Sprinkle the cucumber and carrot evenly over the noodles.

Put all the ingredients for the dressing in a blender and whizz to combine. Pour the dressing over the noodles, top with the shredded chicken and garnish with the coriander. Finally, sprinkle with chilli powder, toss well and serve.

CHENGDU LENG MIAN noodles

Noodles are such a part of Chinese culinary culture that it is hard to imagine that we could be defeated by the weather: despite the hot humid summers of Sichuan, we still eat noodles there, but we eat them cold. They are actually quite refreshing and the spicy hot sauce has a cooling effect on the palate and body. Weather aside, what is more important is that the noodles are tasty and, indeed, these noodles are!

Serves 2–4

450g (1lb) dried or fresh Chinese egg noodles
175g (6oz) fresh beansprouts

For the sauce
2 tablespoons oil, preferably groundnut
2 tablespoons finely chopped spring onions
1 tablespoon finely chopped garlic
1 tablespoon yellow bean sauce
2 teaspoons chilli bean sauce
2 tablespoons sesame paste (or peanut butter)
2 teaspoons finely chopped fresh ginger
1 tablespoon Shaoxing rice wine (or dry sherry)
2 tablespoons light soy sauce
1 tablespoon black rice vinegar (or balsamic vinegar)
2 teaspoons sugar
1 tablespoon chilli oil (see page 264)
1 tablespoon sesame oil

For the garnish
fresh coriander leaves

If you are using dried noodles, cook them according to the instructions on the packet, or boil them for 4–5 minutes. Then cool them in cold water until you are ready to use them. If you are using fresh noodles, boil them for 3–5 minutes, then immerse in cold water and drain.

Blanch the beansprouts in boiling water for a few seconds – just in and out. Drain immediately and set aside.

Heat the oil in a wok or large frying pan until it is hot. Add the spring onions, garlic, yellow bean and chilli sauces, sesame paste (or peanut butter) and ginger and stir-fry for 2 minutes. Add the rice wine (or sherry), soy sauce, vinegar, sugar and the chilli and sesame oils and stir to mix. Allow the sauce to cool thoroughly.

Combine the noodles and beansprouts in a large bowl and mix thoroughly with the sauce, then garnish with the coriander and serve at once.

ANTS CLIMBING TREES

This is supposedly a Sichuan noodle snack dish. Its unusual name came about because the small pieces of minced beef (or pork) coat the mung bean noodles and look like ants climbing trees! It is one of my favourite midnight snacks and is so easy to make if you have the ingredients in your store cupboard. It tastes good, makes a great dish for kids and won't take too much time in the kitchen. To get children to eat their carrots, you can grate some and toss through with the spring onions at the end.

Serves 2

2 tablespoons groundnut oil
2 garlic cloves, peeled, crushed and finely chopped
1 tablespoon freshly grated root ginger
1 medium fresh red chilli, de-seeded and finely chopped
250g (9oz) minced beef (or pork)
1 tablespoon Shaoxing rice wine (or dry sherry)
1 tablespoon dark soy sauce
1 tablespoon chilli bean paste
200ml (7fl oz) hot chicken stock
150g (5oz) mung bean noodles, pre-soaked in hot water
    for 10 minutes, then drained
1 teaspoon toasted sesame oil
2 large spring onions, finely chopped

Heat a wok over high heat and add the groundnut oil. Stir-fry the garlic, ginger and fresh chilli for a few seconds, then add the beef (or pork) and stir-fry for 2–3 minutes until the meat is browned at the edges. Add the rice wine (or sherry), season with the soy sauce and chilli bean paste and mix well.

Add the hot stock and bring to the boil, then add the noodles and stir well.

Season with the sesame oil, then add the spring onions, tossing and mixing all the ingredients well. Serve immediately.

DAN DAN MIAN Spicy Sichuan noodles

Noodles for the Chinese are not simply just a meal, but also a snack to alleviate hunger pangs during the day. This Sichuan dish is a great favourite and certainly has my vote: it is satisfying, quick, easy and absolutely delicious. It's typical of what we Chinese call 'small eats' – which are found in tiny restaurants, food stalls and other enterprising eateries. There are many versions of the dish and they are all easy to make, tasty and quite filling. I love this version, which I first ate at a tiny street restaurant in Chengdu. Be particularly careful when deep-frying in a wok.

Serves 2–4

225g (8oz) minced pork
1 tablespoon light soy sauce
1 teaspoon salt
225ml (8fl oz) groundnut or vegetable oil
350g (12oz) fresh or dried Chinese thin egg noodles
1 tablespoon Sichuan peppercorns, roasted and ground

For the sauce
3 tablespoons finely chopped garlic
2 tablespoons finely chopped fresh ginger
5 tablespoons finely chopped spring onions
2 tablespoons sesame paste (or peanut butter)
2 tablespoons light soy sauce
2 tablespoons chilli oil (see page 264)
1 teaspoon salt
225ml (8fl oz) chicken stock

For the garnish (optional)
1 fresh red hot chilli, de-seeded and shredded

Combine the pork, soy sauce and salt in a small bowl and mix well.

Heat a wok or sauté pan over high heat until it is hot. Add the oil and heat until it is very hot, then deep-fry the pork, stirring with a spatula to break it into small pieces. When the pork is crispy and dry – after about 5–6 minutes – remove it with a slotted spoon and drain on kitchen paper.

Next, make the sauce. Pour the oil from the wok into a strainer over a heatproof bowl, then put back 2 tablespoons into the wok. Reheat the oil, then add the garlic, ginger and spring onions and stir-fry for 30 seconds. Add the sesame paste (or peanut butter), soy sauce, chilli oil, salt and stock and simmer for 4 minutes.

Cook the noodles in a large pot of boiling water, for 2 minutes if they are fresh, or 5 minutes if they are dried. Drain the noodles well in a colander. Divide the noodles between individual bowls or put them into a large soup tureen. Ladle on the sauce, top with the fried pork and Sichuan peppercorns, then garnish with the chilli, if you like, and serve at once.

HUNAN-STYLE SHREDDED PORK
with chillies and black beans on crispy noodles

This dish is about layers of flavour. It has lots of ingredients but the finished dish is worth the effort. Slivers of meat stir-fried with chillies, black beans and leeks is a classic flavour combination found in Hunnan. I love using lean pork (you could also use chicken) with the crispy noodles. Be particularly careful when deep-frying in a wok.

Serves 2 or 4 to share

1 egg white
1 tablespoon cornflour
sea salt and freshly ground white pepper
300g (11oz) pork fillet, sliced into very fine strips
vegetable oil
2 dried mung bean noodle nests (or use 200g/7oz cooked egg noodles)
2 garlic cloves, peeled, crushed and finely chopped
1 tablespoon freshly grated root ginger
1 medium fresh red chilli, de-seeded and finely chopped
2 dried chillies
1 tablespoon fermented black beans, rinsed and crushed
1 tablespoon Shaoxing rice wine (or dry sherry)
½ teaspoon dark soy sauce
1 tablespoon light soy sauce
1 tablespoon Chinese black rice vinegar (or balsamic vinegar)
2 baby leeks, finely sliced
100ml (3½fl oz) chicken stock
1 tablespoon cornflour, blended with 2 tablespoons cold water
1 teaspoon toasted sesame oil

Combine the egg white, cornflour, salt and white pepper in a bowl. Add the pork strips and toss to coat well. Fill a wok less than half full with vegetable oil and heat the oil to 160°C/325°F, or until a tiny piece of the coating browns in 30 seconds. Add the noodle nests (or noodles) and fry until they have puffed up. Spoon out and drain on kitchen paper. Add the pork and fry for 1–2 minutes until golden. Lift out with a slotted spoon and drain any excess oil on kitchen paper.

Strain the oil through a sieve into a heatproof bowl, then return 1 tablespoon of oil to the wok and reheat. Add the garlic, ginger, fresh and dried chillies and the black beans and toss for a few seconds to release the aroma. Then add the pork and season with the rice wine (or sherry), both soy sauces and the vinegar. Add the leeks and stock and toss together until the leeks have softened and the sauce has come to a bubble. Stir in the blended cornflour until the sauce coats the back of a spoon. Season with the sesame oil.

Place the noodle nests on a serving plate, spoon the shredded pork over the top and serve.

CROSSING-THE-BRIDGE NOODLES

Legend has it that a Chinese scholar, when preparing for the Imperial examinations, isolated himself on an island connected to the shore by a long bridge. His devoted wife would deliver carefully prepared meals to him, but was dismayed that they were always cold on arrival. She finally hit upon the technique of keeping a soup very hot by topping it with a thin layer of vegetable oil. Crossing the long bridge with the hot soup, she was then able to drop the other ingredients into the soup kettle, thus cooking them on the spot. Needless to say, her husband passed his exams. Legend or not, this is a wonderful dish that is typical of Chinese culture, illustrating that food is meant to be shared and is an important part of social interaction. You will find this a great dinner party dish.

CROSSING-THE-BRIDGE NOODLES

Serves 4

25g (1oz) Chinese dried black mushrooms, pre-soaked
  in warm water for about 20 minutes until soft and pliable,
  then drained
165g (5½oz) boneless chicken breasts, cut into thinnest
  slices possible
100g (4oz) boneless lean pork fillet, cut into thinnest
  slices possible
100g (4oz) fresh beansprouts
350g (12oz) dried rice noodles, pre-soaked in warm water
  for 15 minutes, then drained thoroughly
4 spring onions, cut into 5cm (2in) pieces)
900ml (1½ pints) chicken stock

For the dipping condiments
5 tablespoons finely chopped spring onions
3 tablespoons chilli bean sauce
2 tablespoons salt, mixed with 2 teaspoons
  roasted and ground Sichuan peppercorns
5 tablespoons light soy sauce
5 tablespoons Hoisin sauce
5 tablespoons yellow bean sauce

Squeeze the excess water out of the mushrooms, then cut off and discard
the woody stems and finely chop the caps.

Arrange the chicken and pork slices on a platter. Place the beansprouts,
mushrooms and rice noodles on another platter. Put the spring onions into a
small bowl and arrange the dipping condiments in small dishes. Warm four
large soup bowls by rinsing them in very hot water.

Bring the chicken stock to a boil in a medium-sized saucepan. Turn the
heat down and keep just simmering. Remove the bowls from the hot water
and dry carefully. Pour the hot broth into each bowl. Place all the meats,
vegetables and dipping condiments in the centre of the table and let each
diner layer the meats, vegetables, and finally, the noodles in the hot broth, in
order of their preference. Ensure that all the meats are thoroughly cooked
through before eating.

Each diner can season the meat and vegetables with the condiments of
their choice and drink the soup at the end.

CHING'S BEIJING-SICHUAN ZHAJIANG NOODLES

Ken and I cooked at a noodle restaurant called Noodle Loft, where the delicious noodles were made by the very talented chefs from the Shaanxi region in northwest China, most famous for its traditional hand-pulled noodles. So I cooked with these noodles and made a *zhajiang mein*, a mixed sauce noodle. It is a classic Beijing dish and very easy to make. There are many different variations, some with more sauce than others, but I like the traditional *zhajiang* noodles, which are slightly drier than other dishes. Instead of using only leeks and ginger as aromatics, I like to add minced garlic, Sichuan peppercorns and chilli oil to the dish, not forgetting a drop of Shaoxing rice wine, thereby fusing the flavours of two of my favourite regional cuisines – Sichuan and Beijing. I have used pork belly. The trick is to fry it in the wok until the fat is slightly crispy. Make sure you drain off and keep the excess oil after cooking the *zhajiang* noodles – this intense soy-flavoured oil is delicious when used to moisten plain jasmine rice.

Serves 2

200g (7oz) plain wheat flour or egg noodles
1 tablespoon sesame oil
1 tablespoon chilli sauce laced with chilli oil (see page 264)
2 tablespoons groundnut oil
1 tablespoon finely chopped garlic
1 tablespoon finely chopped fresh ginger
2 tablespoons diced baby leeks
1 teaspoon Sichuan peppercorns
250g (9oz) pork belly with skin, diced
1 tablespoon Shaoxing rice wine (or dry sherry)
1 tablespoon fragrant oil (ginger and spring onion-infused oil,
    see page 264)
1 tablespoon dark soy sauce
200ml (7fl oz) chicken and pork stock (or just use chicken stock)
3–4 tablespoons wheat flour bean paste (*tian mian jiang*,
    or 2½ tablespoons Hoisin sauce and ½ tablespoon yellow
    bean paste)
2 tablespoons yellow bean paste
½ cucumber, de-seeded and sliced into matchstick strips
2 small red radishes, sliced into matchstick strips

For the garnish
1 spring onion, finely chopped
2 sprigs curly parsley
2 orchid flowers

Cook the noodles according to the instructions on the packet, then drain.
Divide the sesame oil and chilli sauce between two bowls, place the cooked
noodles in the bowls and set aside.

Heat a wok over high heat and add the groundnut oil. Add the garlic, ginger,
leeks and Sichuan peppercorns and toss in the heat for a few seconds. Then add
the pork belly and stir-fry for 1 minute. Add the rice wine (or sherry), fragrant
oil and dark soy sauce and stir-fry for 1 minute. Add the stock, *tian mian jiang* (or
Hoisin sauce) and yellow bean paste and toss together well. Cook for 2 minutes,
stirring until the pork is cooked. Drain off the excess oil through a sieve into a
heatproof bowl and save for later.

Divide the pork mixture between the two bowls and sprinkle on the cucumber
and radish strips. Garnish with the spring onion, parsley and orchids and serve
immediately. Toss all the ingredients well before eating.

STICKY BELLY PORK RICE
wrapped in lotus leaves

This is one of my all-time favourite comfort recipes. Whenever I go to a *dim sum* restaurant, I cannot resist ordering glutinous rice in lotus leaves. The glutinous rice does not contain any gluten – its name describes the glue-like stickiness of the rice. Glutinous rice is used in savoury and sweet dishes in all the different regional Chinese cuisines and it is often served at Chinese festivals. It's also often ground into a powder and mixed with water to make a dough for desserts and dumplings. The rice is popular not only because it provides a great chewy texture when cooked, but because its stickiness is seen as auspicious – for example, on Chinese New Year, *nian gao*, a sweetened sticky rice cake, is served because it is believed that, as a result, you and your family members will stick together, or stay close, for the coming year.

These parcels are delicious on their own or with some stir-fried vegetables. You can make this a vegetarian dish by using shiitake mushrooms and extra-firm, pressed braised dofu (tofu) pieces (known as *dofu gan*), diced carrots and peanuts.

Serves 2–4 to share

1 tablespoon peanut oil

2.5cm (1in) piece fresh root ginger, peeled and grated

2 small shallots, finely chopped

a small handful of dried shrimps, soaked in hot water for 20 minutes, then drained and finely chopped

5 small, dried shiitake mushrooms, soaked in hot water for 20 minutes, then drained and finely chopped

300g (11oz) pork belly, cut into 0.5cm (¼in) square cubes

1 teaspoon Chinese five-spice powder

1 tablespoon Shaoxing rice wine (or dry sherry)

600g (1lb 5oz) cooked glutinous rice (see overleaf)

2 tablespoons light soy sauce

1 tablespoon dark soy sauce

1 teaspoon toasted sesame oil

a pinch of sea salt

freshly ground white pepper

2 dried lotus leaves, soaked in hot water for 20 minutes, then drained

For the garnish

1–2 spring onions, sliced into long strips, then placed in iced water and drained, to make curls

STICKY BELLY PORK RICE
wrapped in lotus leaves continued

Heat a wok over high heat until it begins to smoke, then add the peanut oil. Add the ginger, shallots, chopped shrimps and mushrooms and stir-fry for 1 minute. Add the pork belly and stir-fry to break it up. When the pork begins to brown, stir in the five-spice and rice wine (or sherry). When the wine has almost evaporated, stir in the cooked rice. Once the rice is incorporated, season with both soy sauces, the sesame oil, salt and white pepper and mix well. Remove from the heat.

Pat the lotus leaves dry with kitchen paper. Spoon half of the sticky rice mixture into the centre of one lotus leaf. Fold in the sides (snug, but not tight), fold up the bottom and roll up, then secure with butchers' twine. Repeat with the remaining lotus leaf and rice. Place in a bamboo steamer and steam for 10 minutes until the fragrance has infused.

Remove from the steamer and unwrap the parcels. Serve garnished with the sliced spring onions.

Glutinous rice

Rinse 300g (11oz) glutinous rice in water until the water runs clear in order to remove excess starch. Place in a pan with 600ml (1 pint) water, then bring to a boil, reduce the heat, cover and simmer for 15 minutes. Ensure all the water has evaporated before using.

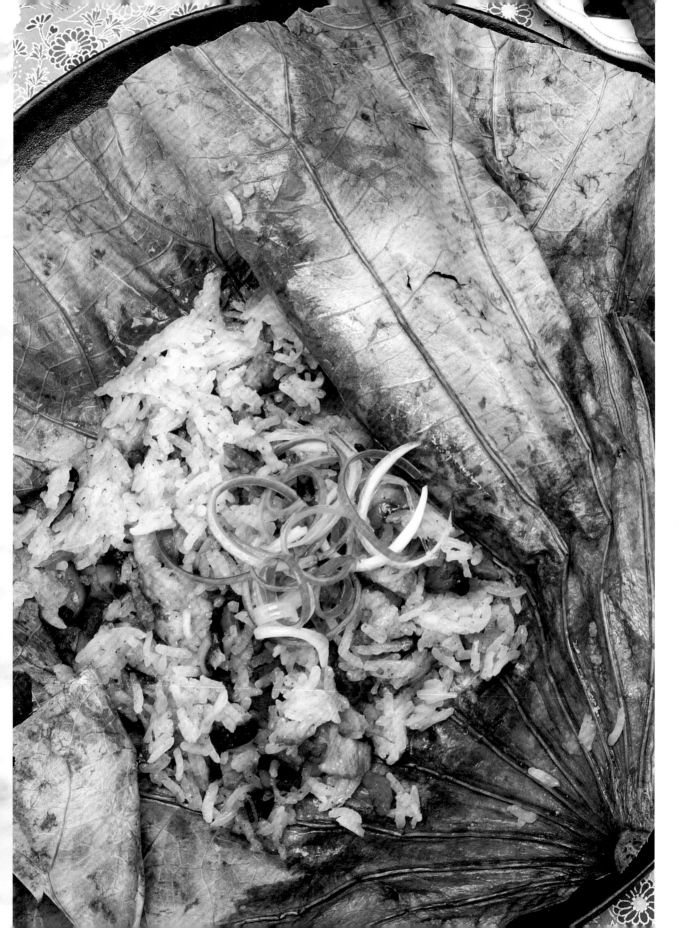

PINEAPPLE RICE

Most people have little idea how vast and diverse a country China is. Yunnan province in southwest China borders on southeast Asia, and I discovered to my joy how similar some of the dishes were to Thai cuisine. This dish combines fruit with a savoury mixture. It makes a delicious change and is easy to make once the rice is cooked.

Serves 4

long grain rice measured to the 400ml (14fl oz) level
   in a measuring jug and cooked
2 tablespoons groundnut or peanut oil
225g (8oz) minced pork
2 tablespoons light soy sauce
salt and freshly ground black pepper
2 tablespoons finely chopped fresh ginger
3 tablespoons finely chopped spring onions
1 tablespoon sesame oil
1 small pineapple, about 225g (8oz), peeled, cored and chopped
   into 1cm (½in) pieces

Allow the cooked rice to cool thoroughly by spreading it out on a baking sheet. The rice must be cold before you use it in this recipe.

Heat a wok over high heat until it is hot. Add the oil, and when it is very hot and slightly smoking, add the pork and stir-fry for 2 minutes. Add the soy sauce, salt, pepper, ginger and spring onions and continue to stir-fry for 2 minutes. Add the rice, mix well and stir-fry the mixture for another 5 minutes until the rice is heated through and well mixed. Stir in the sesame oil, add the pineapple pieces and stir-fry until the pineapple is heated through, but not cooked. Serve at once.

CHING'S BANANA-WRAPPED SMOKED PORK with red and black rice

It was so much fun cooking with Ken on our outdoor balcony in Xishuangbanna in Yunnan. We created a feast! He had bought all the ingredients from a fresh wet market and we improvised, creating a delightful meal to celebrate our time in Yunnan. I was so inspired by the banana leaves used by the Dai women that I decided to wrap a parcel of local smoked *la-rou* (Chinese smoked pork), red shelled peanuts and local spices in the leaves. I then sealed the parcels with toothpicks and steamed them until the rice was cooked through and sticky and fragrant (see page 140). Delicious!

If you can't get hold of the ingredients for the pepper seasoning, use ½ teaspoon of Chinese five-spice powder.

Makes 4

1 teaspoon vegetable oil
a handful of diced smoked pork (or lardons)
100g (4oz) red-shelled peanuts, boiled for 45 minutes, then drained
250g (9oz) each red and black rice, soaked overnight
a pinch of salt
1 tablespoon light soy sauce
2 large banana leaves, each cut in half

For the pepper seasoning
1 tablespoon Yunnan flower peppercorns
2 star anise
2 large black Chinese cardamom pods

Toast the peppercorns, star anise and cardamoms in a wok on medium heat for about 30 seconds, or until they release their aroma. Place in a mortar and pestle and grind (or in a towel and grind using the back of bamboo cleaver, but be careful!).

Heat a wok over high heat and add the vegetable oil. Add the smoked pork and stir-fry for 1 minute. Add half the toasted spices, then stir in the peanuts, rice, salt and light soy sauce and stir-fry for another minute. (You can store the remaining toasted spices in a jar to use another time.)

Divide the mixture between the pieces of banana leaf, wrap up like an envelope and secure each with a toothpick. Place on a heatproof plate in a wok and steam on high heat for 40 minutes until cooked through.

HAINAN CHICKEN RICE

HAINAN CHICKEN RICE

This dish is a wonderful example of the power of food and illustrates how recipes will migrate along with those who enjoy them. It was originally from Hainan Island in the south, where it was made with the famous Wenchang chicken. It is now cooked throughout southeast Asia, especially in Singapore where Chinese immigrants prepare it at home and in their restaurants. Although the method may seem a little laborious, it is well worth the effort, especially if you have a good chicken. Part of the treat is eating it with all the garnishes and sauces, making it a complete meal in itself. The rice is often considered a delicacy on its own – I think you will agree once you have made this recipe.

Serves 4

1 x 1.5kg (3–3½lb) chicken
salt
1.75 litres (3 pints) chicken stock
6 slices of fresh ginger
6 whole spring onions
½ teaspoon freshly ground black pepper
1 tablespoon groundnut or vegetable oil
2 tablespoons finely chopped garlic
long-grain rice measured to the 400ml (14fl oz) level in a measuring jug

For the garnish
450g (1lb) cucumber (about 1 large)
225g (8oz) tomatoes
2 spring onions

For the ginger and spring onion sauce
4 tablespoons finely chopped spring onions, white part only
2 teaspoons finely chopped fresh ginger
1 teaspoon salt
2 tablespoons groundnut or vegetable oil

For the chilli sesame sauce
2 fresh red chillies, de-seeded and finely chopped
2 teaspoons sesame oil
1 teaspoon sugar
½ teaspoon salt

Rub the chicken evenly with 1 tablespoon of salt, then place in a large pot, cover with the stock (adding more stock if necessary) and bring to the boil. Add the ginger, spring onions and pepper, cover tightly, then turn the heat down and simmer gently for 30 minutes. Turn off the heat and leave covered tightly for 1 hour. Remove the chicken from the pot and allow it to cool. Remove the ginger and spring onions with a slotted spoon. Skim off any surface fat from the stock, then measure 900ml (1½ pints) of stock and set it aside – this will be used to cook the rice. Reserve the rest of the stock.

Heat a wok or large frying pan over high heat until it is hot. Add the oil, and when it is very hot and slightly smoking, add the garlic and 1 teaspoon of salt and stir-fry for 1 minute. Add the rice and continue to stir-fry for 2 minutes. Now add the reserved measured stock to the rice, bring the mixture to the boil and continue boiling until most of the liquid has evaporated. Turn the heat to very low and cover tightly. Let the rice cook undisturbed for 15 minutes. Remove the wok from the heat and let the rice rest for 5 minutes before serving.

Meanwhile, prepare the garnish. Peel the cucumber, slice it in half lengthways and, using a teaspoon, remove the seeds. Slice the cucumber. Thinly slice the tomatoes. Slice the spring onions on the diagonal. Arrange all the slices on a platter and set aside.

Next, make the two sauces. Mix the spring onions, ginger and salt together in a heatproof bowl. Heat the wok over high heat until it is very hot. Add the oil, and when it is very hot and slightly smoking, pour it on to the ginger and spring onion mixture and mix well. Combine all the chilli sesame sauce ingredients in a small bowl and mix well.

Transfer the chicken to a chopping board, cut it into bite-sized pieces and arrange it on a platter. Reheat the remaining stock and serve it in a soup tureen. Serve the rice in a bowl with the plate of garnish and the sauces.

FUJIAN AND TAIWAN: Ching's homecoming

None of my family really knows the exact history of my ancestors, but we think we are descended from Han Chinese people who settled in the southwestern province of Fujian (I can speak a Fujian dialect). For centuries, there was a lot of piracy in the South China Sea, and it is thought that pirates took many Fujian people to the nearby island of Taiwan (possibly as slaves, although no-one knows for sure). To start my 'homecoming' journey, I travelled from Xiamen in Fujian to Taiwan, much as I imagine my Han ancestors would have done…

Fujian Province has a long coastline on the South China Sea, and Xiamen (once known as Amoy), is its major port. Xiamen is now a huge and successful city: helped by governmental investment in the 1980s, it has also benefitted, educationally and culturally, from gifts and donations from what is called the 'overseas Chinese' diaspora. Most of the Chinese who have settled all over the world in the last few centuries come from these southern parts of China, from Guangdong, Hong Kong and Fujian. In their new homes these emigrant Chinese have opened restaurants, formed communities, integrated into communities, worked hard, succeeded, and then wanted to give something back. In many ways, it is the overseas Chinese who have been responsible for nurturing the 'real' Chinese culture and keeping it alive. With the Cultural Revolution, when China closed its doors to the rest of the world, many aspects of traditional Chinese culture disappeared from mainland China, and it was only overseas that they survived. Both Ken and I are 'overseas Chinese', from Canton and Taiwan respectively. I hope that we two might also be able to give something back…

However, some of those setting out from Fujian did not go far, and settled much nearer to their original homeland, in Formosa (christened by 16th-century Portuguese 'Ilha Formosa' or 'beautiful isle'), now known as Taiwan. This island, not far from the Fujian coast, has had a tempestuous history: it has belonged variously to the Japanese and Chinese, and became the base of the Republic of China, led by Chiang Kai-shek, after the ROC lost mainland China to the Communists in 1949. At this time, the defeated government took many ancient and priceless Chinese relics with them to Taiwan, where they are still kept. (If they had remained on the mainland during those tumultuous times they would almost certainly have been lost or destroyed during the Cultural Revolution.) It was also in Taiwan that traditional Chinese festivities were nurtured – with Chinese New Year celebrations, dragon boat and autumn boat festivals among them – and these have now begun to filter back to the mainland. Although the two can be said to remain at odds politically, when China introduced its 'open-door' policy in 1979, it was the Taiwanese who came to the mainland, bringing money with them (they were the first to invest in Shanghai, for instance), as well as those wonderful festival traditions.

Taiwan is where I was brought up until I was five years old, and many of my family still live there. I was fortunate to travel back to Kaohsiung in southwestern Taiwan and then on to Bai He, my grandmother's village in southern Taiwan, where I was reunited with my grandfather and our extended family. My visit coincided with the festival of *Qing Ming* – the traditional tomb-sweeping ceremony – in early April, when we burned incense together to pay our respects to our ancestors. Because it's a spring festival, we celebrated by eating a feast of cold food: *lun piah* (fresh spring rolls), cold boiled dofu (tofu), shredded chicken, peanuts and fruit (particularly apples, which are important because they symbolise peace).

These foods are very typically Taiwanese. The island's cooking, however, is inevitably very close to Fujianese, which is considered to be one of the major styles of Chinese cuisine. In fact, Taiwanese cooking could be said to be a fusion of several styles of Chinese cooking: because so many top chefs fled with the Nationalists to Taiwan in 1949, it is probable that the traditional Chinese food culture was able to survive there. There are soups, stews, noodles, dumplings and lots of snacks to be had in the many popular street markets: these include stinky dofu (a fermented dofu/tofu), usually deep-fried outdoors and served with chilli bean sauce and preserved cabbage – it is too smelly to be cooked indoors! Other dishes you might come across are oyster omelettes, salty crispy chicken, and braised pork belly *bao* (all the rage in America at the moment).

But there are also Hakka and Japanese influences on Taiwanese cooking. The Hakkas, a branch of the Han, are numerous on Taiwan, and they have some very distinctive dishes. These include salt-baked chicken, for instance, stuffed duck, and the festive *poon choi*, or 'big basin feast', which includes a wonderful selection of poached meat, fish, shellfish, vegetables and often lotus root (extensive fields of lotus grow in Taiwan). The Japanese ruled Formosa (Taiwan) for over 50 years, and inevitably some influences remain. The Taiwanese eat sashimi and sushi, use wasabi and seaweed, and cook with a rice wine that is more like mirin than the Chinese Shaoxing rice wine. And the Japanese are probably also responsible for the Taiwanese passion for karaoke!

My formal welcoming home was a huge feast with my extended family – some twenty to twenty-five people. We ate a broad range of food that was representative of Taiwanese cuisine. It may have been a bit pot-luck, but we did eat well, and it was so good to see everybody. It was also wonderful to see my grandfather, my last remaining grandparent. After we visited my grandmother's shrine, I cooked lunch for the family. I chose to make the traditional dishes that she used to cook for me when I was a child and that remind me of her: bamboo rice, egg and tomato stir-fry, red bean soup dumplings and clams. I first learned to cook in my grandmother's kitchen and cooking there again – but without her – was incredibly poignant.

VEGETARIAN

STIR-FRIED SPINACH
with chilli-fermented dofu

I grew up in a Chinese household that loved vegetables. We ate meat occasionally, but certainly not for every meal. The variety of vegetables in Chinese cuisine seems so much greater than in Western cuisine. I was always happy to have a savoury, stir-fried vegetable dish with plain rice. The secret lies in the flavouring. The hot wok gives the vegetables a grilled, smoky flavour, while elements like garlic and ginger, together with fermented dofu (tofu), give it a mouth-watering appeal. That is what transforms this dish from ordinary to superb and enticing – and it is not only for vegetarians!

Serves 4 as a side dish

1kg (2lb) fresh Chinese water spinach (or European spinach)
2 tablespoons groundnut or vegetable oil
4 garlic cloves, thinly sliced
2 tablespoons finely chopped fresh ginger
3 tablespoons chilli-fermented or plain dofu (tofu)
2 tablespoons Shaoxing rice wine (or dry sherry)

Wash the Chinese water spinach thoroughly and drain. Cut off and discard 5cm (2in) from the bottom of the stem, which tends to be tough. Cut the rest of the spinach into 7.5cm (3in) segments. If you are using ordinary spinach, wash it thoroughly and remove all the stems, leaving just the leaves.

Heat a wok or large frying pan over high heat until it is hot. Add the oil, and when it is very hot and slightly smoking, add the garlic and ginger and stir-fry for 15 seconds. Then add the dofu and crush it with a spatula, breaking it into small pieces. Add the spinach and stir-fry for 3 minutes. Pour in the rice wine (or sherry) and cook for another 3 minutes. Transfer to a serving platter and serve at once.

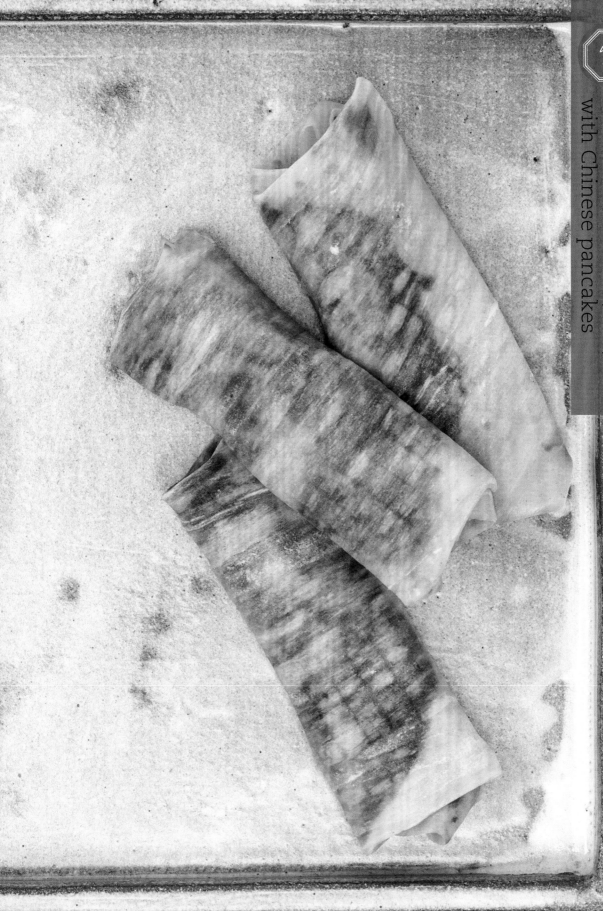

MU SHU VEGETARIAN
with Chinese pancakes

MU SHU VEGETARIAN
with Chinese pancakes

Most people outside China associate our cuisine with rice, but in fact more than half of China thrives on wheat in the form of noodles, steamed bread and crêpe-like wrappings such as pancakes. This is a typical recipe you would find in northern and even western China. Most often you will find this made with either pork or beef. I think my vegetarian version meets the tests of both texture and taste.

Serves 4

25g (1oz) Chinese dried lily stems, soaked for 20 minutes,
    then drained
50g (2oz) Chinese dried tree ear fungus (mushrooms),
    soaked for 20 minutes until soft and pliable, then drained
50g (2oz) Sichuan preserved vegetables, soaked for 20 minutes,
    then drained
3 tablespoons groundnut or vegetable oil
4 eggs, beaten
6 spring onions, finely shredded
1 teaspoon sugar
1 teaspoon salt
1 teaspoon freshly ground black pepper
1 tablespoon Shaoxing rice wine (or dry sherry)
1½ tablespoons light soy sauce
2 teaspoons sesame oil

To serve
1 x recipe Chinese pancakes (opposite)
Hoisin sauce or bean paste, for dipping

Trim off the hard ends of the lily stems and shred them by pulling them apart. Rinse the tree ears in several changes of water, remove the hard stems and shred the tree ears finely. Rinse the preserved vegetables in several changes of water, then shred them finely.

Heat a wok over high heat until it is very hot, then add 1½ tablespoons of the oil. When the oil is very hot, add the eggs and gently stir-fry, lifting them up and around until set. Remove immediately and drain on kitchen paper.

Wipe the wok clean with kitchen paper and reheat it over high heat until very hot. Add the remaining 1½ tablespoons of oil, and when the oil is hot, add the lily stems, tree ears, preserved vegetables and spring onions and stir-fry for 1 minute. Then add the rest of the ingredients and stir-fry for another 2 minutes. Return the eggs to the wok and stir-fry the mixture for another 2 minutes, mixing thoroughly. Serve at once with the Chinese pancakes and Hoisin sauce.

Chinese pancakes

Makes 18

275g (10oz) plain flour, plus extra for dusting
225ml (8fl oz) very hot water
2 tablespoons sesame oil

Put the flour into a large bowl. Stir the hot water gradually into the flour, mixing all the while with chopsticks or a fork, until the water is fully incorporated. Add more water if the mixture seems dry. Then remove the mixture from the bowl and knead it with your hands until smooth. This should take about 8 minutes. Put the dough back into the bowl, cover it with a clean, damp towel and let it rest for about 30 minutes.

After the resting period, take the dough out of the bowl and knead it again for about 5 minutes, dusting with a little flour if it is sticky. Once the dough is smooth, form it into a roll about 46cm (18in) long and about 2.5cm (1in) in diameter. Take a knife and cut the roll into equal segments. There should be about 18. Roll each segment into a ball.

Take two of the dough balls. Dip one side of one ball into the sesame oil and place the oiled side on top of the other ball. Take a rolling pin and roll the two together into a circle about 15cm (6in) in diameter. It is important to roll double pancakes in this way because the resulting dough will remain moist inside, and you will be able to roll them thinner but avoid the risk of overcooking them later.

Heat a frying pan or wok over a very low flame. Put the double pancake into the pan or wok and cook until it has dried on one side. Flip it over and cook the other side until dried. Remove from the pan, gently peel the two pancakes apart and set them aside. Repeat this process until all the dough balls have been cooked.

Steam the pancakes to reheat them, or alternatively you could wrap them tightly in a double sheet of foil and put them into a pan containing 2.5cm (1in) of boiling water. Cover the pan, turn the heat down very low and simmer until they are reheated. Don't be tempted to reheat them in the oven, as this will dry them out too much.

If you want to freeze the cooked pancakes, wrap them tightly in clingfilm first. When using pancakes that have been frozen, thaw them in the fridge first before reheating them.

LOTUS ROOT AND WOOD EAR FUNGUS

in soy sesame dressing tossed in finely chopped coriander

Lotus roots are used in many Chinese dishes. They can be eaten cold in a salad, like this one, but to prepare them you need to blanch them in boiling water and then finely slice them. They are sweet and crunchy and have a delicate flavour – a cross between water chestnuts and bamboo. They are delicious in this simple soy sesame dressing paired with crunchy wood ear mushrooms – very refreshing on a hot summer's day as the perfect *leng cai*, or cold appetiser.

Serves 2 as a side dish

2 fresh lotus roots (vacuum-packed), peeled and blanched in hot water for 2 minutes, then drained and sliced using a mandolin

50g (2oz) Chinese dried black wood ear mushrooms, pre-soaked in warm water for 20 minutes, then drained and finely sliced

2 tablespoons light soy sauce

2 tablespoons toasted sesame oil

2 tablespoons Chinese clear (plain) rice vinegar (or cider vinegar)

a small handful of fresh coriander, very finely chopped

1 teaspoon chilli oil (see page 264)

Toss the lotus roots and mushrooms together in a bowl with the soy sauce, sesame oil and vinegar and chill for 15 minutes.

To serve, toss the chopped coriander through the mixture and drizzle with chilli oil.

Note: Instead of lotus root, you could use finely sliced tinned water chestnuts and blanched shiitake mushrooms.

BRAISED SAVOURY TREE EARS

Sichuan is ideal territory for mushrooms, as the climate there is warm and moist, which they love. So, naturally, fungi dishes appear on menus everywhere. I was delighted to discover this dish by accident during our filming in Chengdu. After an intensive morning in the spice market, we were all famished and simply popped into the nearest restaurant. Of the procession of many dishes, this one stood out. Dried tree ears were stir-fried and braised in spicy chilli-fermented dofu (tofu) and the result was a vegetarian dish of uncommon deliciousness.

Serves 4

150g (5oz) Chinese dried tree ear fungus (mushrooms), soaked in boiling water
    for 20 minutes, then drained
1½ tablespoons groundnut or vegetable oil
3 tablespoons coarsely chopped garlic
1 tablespoon finely chopped fresh ginger
3 tablespoons chilli-fermented dofu (tofu)
2 teaspoons sugar
salt and freshly ground black pepper
1 tablespoon Shaoxing rice wine (or dry sherry)
1½ tablespoons light soy sauce
50ml (2fl oz) vegetable or chicken stock (or water)
3 tablespoons finely chopped spring onions
2 teaspoons sesame oil
1½ teaspoons roasted and ground Sichuan peppercorns

Rinse the tree ears well in water, then drain again.

Heat a wok or large frying pan over high heat until it is hot. Add the oil, and when it is very hot and slightly smoking, add the garlic and ginger and stir-fry for 30 seconds. Add the fermented dofu and crush it in the wok, then add the tree ears and stir-fry, mixing well, for a few minutes. Quickly add the sugar, salt, pepper, rice wine (or sherry), soy sauce and stock (or water). Turn the heat down, cover and cook gently for about 20 minutes, stirring from time to time until the tree ears have absorbed most of the liquid. Turn the heat back to high and continue to cook until most of the liquid has been reduced. Then mix in the spring onions and stir for a few seconds.

Drizzle with the sesame oil, sprinkle the Sichuan peppercorns over and serve at once.

STIR-FRIED SWISS CHARD

This recipe was inspired by a visit to Chef Yu Bo, one of the rising top chefs in China who has modernised Sichuan cooking with his own personal twist. I went with him to an organic farm near Chengdu to pick fresh greens to cook. Although the vegetable he picked is not available outside of Sichuan, I found Swiss chard to be quite similar and to work just as well. However, Chef Yu Bo did have a secret ingredient: a 10-year-old chilli bean paste redolent with deep flavours of garlic, chilli and broad beans – rich but incredibly fragrant at the same time. I managed to duplicate a version – not quite like his, but delicious, nevertheless.

Serves 4

450g (1lb) Swiss chard (or Chinese water spinach), stalks and leaves separated
1½ tablespoons groundnut or vegetable oil
2 tablespoons chilli bean paste
2 tablespoons finely chopped fresh ginger
2 teaspoons sugar
salt and freshly ground black pepper
4 tablespoons finely chopped spring onions
5 tablespoons finely chopped celery heart
4 tablespoons finely chopped fresh coriander

With a sharp knife, remove any tough fibres from the chard (or spinach) stalks. Wash thoroughly, then chop coarsely into fairly large chunks and set aside.

Heat a wok or large frying pan over high heat until it is hot. Add the oil, and when it is very hot and slightly smoking, add the chilli bean paste and ginger and stir-fry for 1 minute until it is fragrant. Then add the Swiss chard (or spinach) stalks and stir-fry for 2 minutes. Add the leaves and stir-fry for 3 minutes until wilted. Season with sugar, salt and pepper.

Finally, stir in the spring onions, celery heart and coriander and stir-fry for another minute. Turn on to a platter and serve at once.

BUDDHA'S MIXED STIR-FRIED VEGETABLES with cashews

Sometimes a plate of stir-fried vegetables is enough to make you feel whole again – there is nothing more satisfying than a plate of greens to make you healthy! I love making a simple stir-fry sauce using vegetarian oyster sauce (made from mushrooms), light soy and good-quality stock – the one shown here is an all-purpose stir-fry sauce that I use to season vegetables or meat. This dish is simple and so tasty – make the sauce, keep to one side, stir-fry the ingredients, add the sauce, and Bob's your uncle! You can use any vegetables that are in season, but make sure that as you stir-fry you keep the vegetables *al dente* to retain their nutritional value and delicious flavours.

Serves 2–4 to share

1 tablespoon groundnut oil
1 tablespoon freshly grated root ginger
1 carrot, peeled and sliced into long, thin julienne strips
5 fresh shiitake mushrooms, sliced
a small handful of baby corn, sliced in half
1 x 225g tin bamboo shoots, drained and sliced into long, thin julienne strips
a handful of roasted, salted cashew nuts
a small handful of beansprouts
2 spring onions, sliced on the diagonal

For the sauce
100ml (3½fl oz) cold vegetable stock
1 tablespoon light soy sauce
1 tablespoon vegetarian oyster sauce
1 teaspoon toasted sesame oil
1 tablespoon cornflour

Combine all the ingredients for the sauce in a bowl, then put to one side.

Heat a wok over high heat and add the groundnut oil. Add the ginger and stir-fry for a few seconds. Tip in the carrot, mushrooms, baby corn and bamboo shoots and stir-fry for 2 minutes. Add the sauce to the wok and bring to the boil. Add the cashew nuts and toss together. When the sauce has thickened, reduce the heat and add the beansprouts and spring onions, toss well and cook for less than 1 minute. Transfer to a serving plate and serve, with jasmine rice.

CHING   Vegetarian

CHING'S VEGETARIAN MAPO DOFU

with *jiang dou* (Chinese long bean) and shredded pickled bamboo in chilli oil

In Chengdu Ken and I had the pleasure of visiting a 'fly' restaurant recommended by our friend Jenny Gao. Fly restaurants are so-called because they are usually hole-in-the-wall places found in alleyways (or are difficult to find) but their food is so good that people swarm around them – like flies to good food! Ken and I had such fun. We tried the water-cooked carp – slices of carp flash-fried in oil so they are super tender. A layer of local vegetables is placed on the bottom of a dish, the carp is layered on top then Sichuan pepper and ground dried Sichuan chilli flakes are sprinkled over the entire dish. Hot sizzling oil is added, which turns the dish a blood red. Fierce, strong and spicy, it had us reaching for the *bai jiou* (distilled white liquor), which is robust enough to cleanse the palate between mouthfuls of *mala* (numbing spicy heat). In the end we probably drank too much *bai jiou*, but I realised that one cannot really have enough *bai jiou*, even at 52 per cent alcohol volume!

We also tried dishes like tender rabbit cubes stir-fried with green chillies (which were mild and slightly spicy), garnished with a thread of green flower peppercorns native to Yunnan (Sichuan's neighbour). The delicious *la-rou* was another dish we sampled – this was a front shoulder of pork, which was tea-smoked, then wrapped in lotus leaves and steamed.

Then came the famed Old (pockmarked) Mrs. Chen's *dofu* (tofu). It was the classic reddish-brown, numbingly spicy, delicious wobbly *dofu* but with… wait for it… pigs' brains! It was the first and the last time for me. I am Chinese and I do love offal, from pigs' ears to the intestines, but I draw the line at brains. Ken, on the other hand, loved it! But he's Cantonese and they eat everything. I did enjoy the dofu though, and we then convinced the head chef to show us his version of the classic *mapo dofu*. First he bathed small cubes of dofu in hot water and added a pinch of salt to 'open it up to flavours', then he drained the cloudy water and set the dofu aside. He heated a combination of lard and chilli oil in a hot wok and added chilli bean paste, fermented black beans, chilli paste (using pickled chillies), minced garlic and ginger to the wok to 'explode' in the hot oil. He then added half a ladleful of minced pork belly and tossed the ingredients together. He poured in some cooking wine, followed by a quarter cup of water, then seasonings of light soy sauce and black rice vinegar. He added the dofu and tossed it together, then added cornflour to thicken the sauce.

Then he tossed in a large handful of *suan miao* (the dark green, tougher part of the Chinese leek, cut into 1cm/½in slices). Then, with a final toss, it was on the plate and a few pinches of toasted and ground Sichuan peppercorns were sprinkled over the top. The lesson was over and then it was our turn to make our version of the same dish! Ken made a delicious vegetarian version with Sichuan preserved vegetables, which gave the dish a briny-sour taste, increasing its umami flavour.

I also made a vegetarian version of *mapo dofu*, except I used pickled bamboo shoots in chilli oil and *jiang dou*, the local Sichuan long bean, which I thought gave the dish extra crunch and complemented the soft dofu well, adding texture and *kou-gan* (mouth-feel) to the dish. (I've also made a beef version, see page 185.)

Serves 2–4 to share

500ml (17fl oz) water
250g (9oz) fresh silken dofu (tofu), sliced into 1cm (½in) cubes
1–2 tablespoons vegetable oil
150g (5oz) *jiang dou* (or French beans), cut into 1cm (½in) pieces
100g (4oz) pickled sour bamboo shoots in chilli oil (or pickled cornichons), cut into 1cm (½in) pieces
1 tablespoon cornflour blended with 2 tablespoons cold water
2 pinches of toasted and ground Sichuan peppercorns

For the sauce
1 teaspoon minced garlic
1 teaspoon minced fresh ginger
1 teaspoon fermented salted black beans, rinsed
1 tablespoon chilli bean paste
1 tablespoon light soy sauce
1 tablespoon Chinese black rice vinegar (or balsamic vinegar)
1 tablespoon Shaoxing rice wine (or dry sherry)
200ml (7fl oz) water

Heat a wok over high heat. Add the water and heat, then add the dofu pieces and swirl in the water for about 1 minute (to 'clean' the dofu). Drain and set to one side.

Reheat the wok over high heat and add 1 tablespoon of vegetable oil. Combine all the ingredients for the sauce except the water, then add to the wok to 'explode' in the heat. Add a little more oil if necessary. Add the beans and pickled bamboo pieces (or cornichons) and toss together well. Then add the water and bring to the boil. Return the dofu to the wok and mix well. As the sauce bubbles, add the blended cornflour and stir in to thicken the sauce. Transfer to a serving plate and garnish with the ground peppercorns. Serve immediately with jasmine rice.

KEN'S MAPO DOFU
vegetarian style

Mapo dofu (pockmarked tofu) is probably as well known in China as fish and chips are in the UK. Legend has it that Old Mrs Chen, who was nicknamed 'Pockmarked Chen' for the marks on her face, opened an inexpensive restaurant in Chengdu and served this dish in response to the restaurant competition on her street. Whatever the reason, it is a brilliant way to blend spicy, peppery, hot, tender, fresh and fragrant ingredients into a classic dish.

I have taken the meat out of the recipe and made an equally tasty vegetarian version, which I know you will love.

Serves 4

100g (4oz) Sichuan preserved vegetables,
   soaked for 20 minutes, then drained
2 tablespoons groundnut or vegetable oil
2 tablespoons coarsely chopped garlic
1 tablespoon whole yellow bean sauce
1 tablespoon dark soy sauce
salt and finely ground black pepper
1–2 teaspoons red chilli powder
150ml (¼ pint) vegetable stock
450g (1lb) fresh soft or silken dofu (tofu),
   cut into 2.5cm (1in) cubes
2 teaspoons cornflour, mixed with 1 tablespoon water

For the garnish
1 tablespoon Sichuan peppercorns, roasted
   and finely ground

Rinse the preserved vegetables in several changes of water, then mince finely. Heat a wok or large sauté pan until it is hot. Add the oil, and when it is hot, add the garlic and stir-fry for 20 seconds, then add the preserved vegetables and continue to stir-fry for another 30 seconds. Then add the yellow bean sauce, soy sauce and salt and pepper and stir-fry for another minute. Add the chilli powder and stir-fry for 30 seconds, then pour in the stock, add the dofu and cook for 3 minutes. Stir in the cornflour mixture and cook for another minute.

Ladle the mixture into a serving bowl, garnish with the ground Sichuan peppercorns and serve at once.

AUBERGINE WITH SESAME SAUCE

Chengdu in Sichuan province gets extremely hot and humid in the summer and, as a result, many of the residents tend to eat room-temperature dishes, rather than hot, stir-fried ones. Normally, the Sichuanese cooks would fry the aubergine in a wok (because of the lack of ovens in the home) but I found the traditional method too heavy and greasy for my taste. However, by cooking the aubergine first in the oven and then adding the sauce, I have kept the spirit of Sichuan alive in the dish. It makes a lovely side vegetable dish or a main dish with rice.

Serves 4

675g (1½lb) Chinese aubergine (or regular aubergines)

For the sauce
3 tablespoons sesame paste (or peanut butter)
2 teaspoons roasted and ground Sichuan peppercorns
2 tablespoons sesame oil
2 teaspoons chilli oil (see page 264)
1 tablespoon sugar
1 tablespoon finely chopped garlic
salt and freshly ground black pepper
1 tablespoon chilli bean sauce
2 teaspoons sesame oil
3 tablespoons finely chopped fresh coriander

For the garnish
fresh coriander leaves

Preheat the oven to 200°C/400°F/gas 6. Put the aubergines into a roasting tin and bake them, for about 35 minutes if they are the Chinese variety or 50 minutes if they are the larger variety. They should be charred outside and tender inside. Allow them to cool thoroughly, then peel them. Set aside until you are ready to use them.

When you are ready to serve the dish, combine all the sauce ingredients together with the cooked aubergines and mix well. Garnish with the coriander leaves and serve at room temperature.

RED-COOKED BUTTERNUT SQUASH

This is a simple but delicious dish that can be served as an accompaniment or as a main vegetarian dish alongside vegetables. 'Red-cooked' is a term used in Chinese cuisine to describe a sauce that uses light and dark soy, sugar and spices (such as star anise) to create a deep reddish-brown braising liquid to flavour meat, fish or eggs. This is a quick red-cooked dish using butternut squash; the result is a sweet and savoury, spiced dish.

Serves 2-4 to share

1 medium butternut squash, halved lengthways and peeled
1 tablespoon peanut oil
2.5cm (1in) piece fresh root ginger, peeled and grated
3 star anise
2 cinnamon sticks, about 7.5cm (3in) each
4 tablespoons light soy sauce
2 tablespoons dark soy sauce
250ml (9fl oz) hot water
a pinch of Chinese five-spice powder
1 heaped tablespoon brown sugar

For the garnish
a small handful of fresh coriander

Scoop out and discard the seeds from the squash and cut the flesh into bite-sized (2.5cm/1in) pieces.

Heat a wok over medium-high heat, then add the peanut oil. Add the ginger, star anise and cinnamon and stir-fry for a few seconds, then add the squash and stir-fry for 1 minute. Season with both soy sauces and stir-fry for 1 minute. Add the hot water and stir to combine. Cover the wok and cook, stirring occasionally, until the squash is tender – about 10 minutes. Add more water if necessary to keep the squash from sticking to the sides of the wok. Season with the five-spice and brown sugar and toss well. Remove from the heat and stir to combine. Garnish with the coriander, then serve.

STIR-FRIED CORN AND CHILLI

I am constantly amazed at the influence of history on the culture of food and the migration of certain dishes and customs as populations move. A tiny country like Portugal was responsible for spreading the foods of the New World to China in the 16th century. Foods such as corn, chillies and peanuts until then were totally unknown to the Chinese. Yet here is a simple, home-cooked recipe that is satisfyingly delicious and easy to make.

Serves 4 as a side dish

275g (10oz) fresh (about 2 ears) or frozen corn
1½ tablespoons groundnut or vegetable oil
salt and freshly ground white pepper
2 large fresh red chillies, de-seeded and finely chopped
1 teaspoon sugar
50ml (2fl oz) vegetable or chicken stock

If the corn is fresh, cut the kernels off the cob. Blanch frozen corn for 5 seconds in boiling water and drain.

Heat a wok or large sauté pan over high heat until it is hot. Add the oil, salt, corn and chillies and stir-fry for 1 minute. Add the pepper, sugar and stock and continue to cook for 3 minutes. Serve at once.

BATTERED SHIITAKE AND OKRA
with citrus five-spice salt

This is a great way to make vegetables tasty – coat them in a rich batter and then deep-fry until crisp and serve with a five-spice salt. To make your own citrus five-spice, dry toast the whole spices in a hot pan or wok for a few seconds to release their oils and aroma and then grind them in a spice grinder – the perfect seasoning for vegetables, fish and meat.

Serve 2–4 to share

2 egg yolks
100g (4oz) potato flour (starch)
2–3 tablespoons cold water (if necessary)
sea salt and freshly ground white pepper
vegetable oil, for deep-frying
6 large fresh shiitake mushrooms
200g (7oz) okra, sliced down the middle on the diagonal

For the citrus five-spice salt
1 tablespoon fennel seeds
1 tablespoon star anise
2 tablespoons Sichuan peppercorns
1 tablespoon cloves
1 cassia bark
2 pieces of dried tangerine peel
1 tablespoon coarse sea salt

Heat a wok over medium heat, then add all the ingredients for the citrus five-spice except the salt and dry-toast for 1 minute to release all the oils and flavours. Transfer to a pestle and mortar or spice grinder and grind until fine. (If using a pestle and mortar, you might want to pass the spice mixture through a fine sieve.) Combine 1 tablespoon of the spice mix with the salt in a bowl, mix well and transfer to a small pinch pot. (Store the remainder in a glass jar and use to season fish or meats, or in marinades.)

Put the egg yolks, potato flour and water into a bowl and mix to a rough batter (not smooth) – the amount of water you use will depend on the size of the eggs. Season with salt and pepper.

Half-fill a wok with vegetable oil, then heat the oil to 180°C/350°F, or until a cube of bread turns golden brown in 15 seconds. Dip the mushrooms and okra pieces into the batter, then fry for 2 minutes, or until golden brown. Remove with a slotted spoon and drain on kitchen paper. Season with the citrus five-spice salt while the vegetables are still hot, then transfer to a serving plate and serve.

STIR-FRIED CABBAGE

Hong Ying, a well-known writer and a great cook, invited me to cook with her in Beijing. It was an irresistible offer that I could not refuse. We went together to her local, colourful market that was as stocked as generously as any you would find in the West. I found a beautiful head of cabbage, a real staple in Beijing kitchens, and some lovely dried shrimp (found in Chinese grocers or supermarkets), which inspired me to cook this dish. Since Hong Ying is from Sichuan, I naturally found some chilli bean paste, which I threw into the dish together with some gin she happened to have handy.

Serves 4

1½ tablespoons groundnut or peanut oil
3 tablespoons coarsely chopped garlic
50g (2oz) dried shrimps, coarsely chopped
450g (1lb) savoy cabbage, halved, cored and cut into 5cm (2in) thick strips
2 tablespoons chilli bean sauce
2 tablespoons gin (or Shaoxing rice wine or dry sherry)
300ml (½ pint) room temperature chicken stock (or water)
salt and freshly ground white pepper,

Heat a wok or large frying pan over high heat until it is hot. Add the oil, and when it is very hot and slightly smoking, add the garlic and dried shrimps and stir-fry for 30 seconds. Then add the cabbage and stir-fry for 5 minutes. Next, add the chilli bean sauce and gin (wine or sherry), stir in the stock (or water) and season with salt and pepper. Continue to cook for 10 minutes, or until the cabbage is tender. Serve at once.

LIQUN ROAST DUCK RESTAURANT'S STIR-FRIED LETTUCE

I was surprised and enchanted by this simple dish, which I ate at one of the best Peking duck restaurants in Beijing. After sampling the famous and fantastic duck with condiments, I tried their other dishes. This one was unexpected and outstanding – crispy lettuce stir-fried, instead of blanched as it would be in Guangzhou. The result was a mouthwatering dish that I could have quite happily eaten just with rice as a main course.

Serves 2–4

1½ tablespoons groundnut or vegetable oil
salt and freshly ground black pepper
½ teaspoon roasted and ground Sichuan peppercorns
4 tablespoons coarsely chopped garlic
675g (1½lb) iceberg or cos lettuce, leaves separated
4 tablespoons oyster sauce (or vegetarian oyster sauce)
3 tablespoons finely chopped spring onions

Heat a wok or large frying pan over high heat until it is hot. Add the oil and when it is slightly smoking, add the salt, pepper, Sichuan peppercorns and garlic and stir-fry for 15 seconds. Then add the lettuce leaves and stir-fry for 1 minute, or until they have wilted slightly. Add the oyster sauce and mix thoroughly, then add the spring onions. Transfer to a serving dish and serve at once.

VEGETARIAN DELIGHT

Vegetarian cooking in China is not one-dimensional. Rather it tends to materialise into delicious tasty dishes with many textures, such as this one. Although it has quite a few ingredients, it is easy and simple to make. It may convert even the most die-hard meat eater!

Serves 4

25g (1oz) Chinese dried black mushrooms, pre-soaked in warm water for about
    20 minutes until soft and pliable, then drained
6 eggs, beaten
1 teaspoon salt
2 teaspoons sesame oil
3 tablespoons groundnut or vegetable oil
1 small onion, peeled and sliced
2 tablespoons finely chopped fresh ginger
2 tablespoons finely sliced garlic
15g (½oz) cloud ear fungus (mushrooms), pre-soaked in warm water
    for 20 minutes, then drained and rinsed well
125g (4½oz) pressed dofu (tofu), cut into thin strips
50g (2oz) bean thread noodles, pre-soaked in warm water
    for 15 minutes, then drained well
225g (8oz) cucumber, peeled, de-seeded and cut into thin strips
3 tablespoons light soy sauce
2 tablespoons yellow bean sauce
3 tablespoons Shaoxing rice wine (or dry sherry)
1 tablespoon Hoisin sauce
2 teaspoons sesame oil

Squeeze the excess water out of the mushrooms, then cut off and discard the woody stems and finely shred the caps into thin strips. Set aside.

Combine the eggs, salt and sesame oil in a small bowl and set aside.

Heat a wok or large frying pan over high heat until it is hot. Add 1½ tablespoons of the oil, and when it is very hot and slightly smoking, turn the heat down to moderate. Add the egg mixture and stir-fry for a few minutes, or until the egg has barely set. Remove the egg from the wok and drain on kitchen paper.

Wipe the wok clean with kitchen paper and reheat it. When it is hot, add the remaining 1½ tablespoons of oil. When it is very hot and slightly smoking, quickly add the onion, ginger and garlic and stir-fry for 2 minutes. Then add the black mushrooms, cloud ears, pressed dofu, bean thread noodles and cucumber and stir-fry for 2 minutes. Add the soy sauce, yellow bean sauce, rice wine (or sherry), Hoisin sauce and sesame oil and stir-fry for 3 minutes. Then add the cooked eggs and stir-fry for 1 minute. Turn out on to a serving platter and serve at once.

STIR-FRIED BITTER MELON
with black bean sauce

This recipe is one of my favourites, partly because it brings back childhood memories of the fragrance of black bean sauce mixed with garlic that often greeted me at the door. So it was natural for me to cook this dish for my family in Kaiping, as it evoked the memory of my mother and her home cooking. I was thrilled that my family loved it.

Serves 4

700g (1½lb) bitter melon, halved lengthways and de-seeded
1 tablespoon groundnut or vegetable oil
100g (4oz) fresh mild red chillies, halved, de-seeded and finely sliced
1 tablespoon finely chopped fresh ginger
2 tablespoons finely chopped garlic
2 tablespoons finely chopped shallots
2 tablespoons finely chopped spring onions
3 tablespoons black beans, coarsely chopped
2 teaspoons sugar
2 tablespoons Shaoxing rice wine (or dry sherry)
150ml (¼ pint) chicken stock or water

For the garnish
1 tablespoon sesame oil

Cut the melon into fine slices and blanch in a pot of boiling water for 2 minutes. Remove with a slotted spoon and drain well on kitchen paper.

Heat a wok or large frying pan over high heat until it is hot. Add the oil, and when it is hot and slightly smoking, add the chillies, ginger, garlic, shallots, spring onions and black beans and stir-fry for 2 minutes. Then add the bitter melon, sugar and rice wine (or sherry) and stock. Bring the mixture to the boil, then reduce the heat to medium. Cover the wok or pan and simmer for 8 minutes, or until the melon is cooked and tender. Drizzle in the sesame oil, turn onto a dish and serve at once.

MME CHENG'S STIR-FRIED SHREDDED POTATOES

Potatoes rarely appeared on my mother's table except in braised dishes. So I was surprised when I met Xingyun Chen, the stylish aunt of our friend Jenny Gao, who is a superb cook, and she served a stir-fried potato dish. Her secret was to cut the potatoes into fine shreds, so that they needed only a small amount of cooking and retained a delightful crunch. It was so good that I greedily very nearly ate the entire lot myself. For a dish like this, I could even consider becoming a vegetarian.

Serves 4

450g (1lb) potatoes, peeled and thinly sliced
salt and freshly ground black pepper
1 tablespoon groundnut or vegetable oil
3 tablespoons coarsely chopped garlic
2 tablespoons finely chopped fresh ginger
2 tablespoons finely chopped pickled ginger
2 tablespoons de-seeded and finely chopped fresh red chillies
2 teaspoons sugar
2 tablespoons Shaoxing rice wine (or dry sherry)
2 teaspoons chilli oil (see page 264)
1½ teaspoons roasted and ground Sichuan peppercorns

Stack the potato slices and cut them into matchsticks. Soak them in a bowl of cold water with 1 teaspoon salt for 5 minutes, then drain thoroughly and blot them dry with kitchen paper.

Heat a wok or large frying pan over high heat until it is hot. Add the oil, and when it is very hot and slightly smoking, add the garlic, the fresh and pickled gingers and the chillies and stir-fry for about 30 seconds. Season with salt and pepper, then add the potatoes and gently stir-fry for 1 minute or so until they are well coated with the spices and flavourings. Add the sugar and rice wine (or sherry) and continue to stir-fry gently over a high heat for 5 minutes, or until most of the water has evaporated and the potatoes are cooked. At this point, add the chilli oil, sprinkle on the peppercorns and serve at once.

CHING'S PU-ER TEA-LEAF OMELETTE
for monks in Yunnan

The Bulang girls, both nicknamed Xiao-Yu (see page 133), took me to their village monastery and I made a fresh pu-er tea omelette for the monks. In return, one of them said a prayer for us and gave us his blessings. It was a really special experience for me.

Serves 2

2 tablespoons vegetable oil
7 eggs, beaten
6 pu-er tea leaves (or fresh sweet basil), finely chopped
2 pinches of salt

Heat a wok over high heat, and as the wok starts to smoke, add the vegetable oil.

Quickly add the beaten eggs, pu-er tea leaves and salt and stir to scramble, then let the egg set into an omelette (take off the heat if it gets too hot). Fry until the egg is cooked and golden brown, flipping it over halfway through to ensure even cooking. Take off the heat, cut into pieces and eat immediately.

Pu-er tea

The pu-er tea that most people will be familiar with is the aged, fermented pu-er, which makes a reddish, light brown brew, but if you use green, unfermented pu-er leaves (which make a light yellow brew), they will give a better result in this dish. However, if you can't get fresh pu-er tea leaves, then use fresh sweet basil instead.

STIR-FRIED TOMATO WITH EGG

Of course, the tomato is not Chinese in origin, although we would have loved to have claimed that it was. Instead, it comes from the New World, and was probably brought to China via Portuguese traders.

The Chinese have taken to tomatoes, like the rest of the world, and although it is officially classified as a fruit, the Chinese, like the Europeans, treat the tomato as a vegetable and would swear emphatically that this is a Chinese tradition. So, frequently, it is stir-fried, in this case with eggs. It makes a quick, easy and satisfying everyday dish.

Serves 2–4

6 eggs, beaten
2 teaspoons sesame oil
salt and freshly ground white pepper
6 spring onions
1½ tablespoons groundnut or vegetable oil
450g (1lb) fresh tomatoes, cut into quarters and then into eighths

Combine the eggs with the sesame oil and salt to taste in a medium-sized bowl, then set aside.

With the flat side of a cleaver or knife, crush the spring onions and then finely shred them.

Heat a wok or large pan until it is hot. Add the oil, spring onions, salt and pepper and stir-fry for 30 seconds. Then add the tomatoes and eggs and cook, stirring continuously, until the eggs are set – about 5 minutes. Quickly place on a platter and serve at once.

YUNNAN and the Chinese minorities

I have been many times to southern China, mostly of course to Taiwan, where I was raised, but I had not visited Yunnan before. I had heard many good things, but didn't quite know what to expect. When we arrived, it really felt as though we were in the tropics, especially after the freezing, damp cold of Sichuan. As soon as we got off the plane, Ken stripped off his shirt to enjoy the sunshine!

Yunnan lies in the far southwest of China, bordering externally on Myanmar (Burma), Laos and Vietnam, and internally with the Tibet Autonomous Region (briefly, to the north), Sichuan, Guizhou and Guangxi. The name 'Yunnan' means 'south of the clouds', and the province ranges from the northern snow-capped mountains to the steamy humidity of tropical forests in the south. There is a rich variety of animal and plant life, and Xishuangbanna, where we stayed while filming, is home to the last few Asian elephants in China.

Probably because of its geographical position, Yunnan has the highest number of ethnic minorities in the whole of China. At least 25 minority groups of the 56 in China are represented: in the south they are related to Thais and Laotians; further north, they are mainly Tibeto-Burmese. Each group has its own spoken language, cuisine, belief systems, festivals and modes of dress. Over the centuries, migrants from the more crowded east, persuaded by government or compelled by invading forces, came to the more sparsely populated Yunnan. These people were mainly Han Chinese, who constitute over 90 per cent of the population of the People's Republic of China (and are the largest single ethnic group in the world). I was lucky enough to experience some of the Dai and Bulang cultures in Yunnan during our trip, and discovered that the region boasts some of the most colourful and spectacular festivals and traditions specific to each group – a really wonderful sight to see.

As you might expect, Yunnanese cuisine is very varied, a mix of the cooking styles of the Han majority and of the resident minorities, and very much influenced by the varying climates. In the north, the cooking is mainly Tibetan in style, with lots of meat (beef, pork, lamb and yak) made into hotpots and curries. There are quite a few mushroom dishes too, because so many wild fungi grow in the mountains. Surprisingly, in a country that does not have much dairy, cow's, goat's and yak's milk cheeses are made by the Bai minority. An acquired taste, yak butter tea, a staple of these cold northern parts, is said to keep you warm, enhance the circulation and skin, and fight fatigue.

In the south, the Dai are Southern Buddhist and so many (but not all) of their dishes are vegetarian, using rice, noodles, vegetables, dofu (tofu), and perhaps some fish.

Insects such as grasshoppers, cockroaches and bamboo 'worms' (really caterpillars) are occasionally eaten, as they are rich in protein. The local bamboo is used in many ways: as building material (for houses, bridges and scaffolding), as cooking vessels, as a preserving medium, and to make bags, trays and plates… One of the most famous Dai dishes is sticky rice roasted in the hollow stalk of a piece of bamboo.

Rice has multiple uses too: apart from being steamed and eaten, it is made into rice cakes, rice noodles, paper (for lamps, books and art), and wine. Pineapple rice is sticky white (or black) rice cooked with coconut milk and pineapple, sometimes even served in a hollowed-out half pineapple. And 'crossing-the-bridge' noodles is perhaps the most famous Yunnan dish: a clear chicken soup with rice noodles, slivers of dofu (tofu), vegetables and meat, seasoned with chilli and onion (see page 72 for Ken's recipe and an explanation of the curious name). Because Yunnan is so close to Thailand, the food almost feels southeast Asian rather than Chinese, in that they use a lot of chillies, fresh Thai mint and coriander. Ken and I had a wonderful time cooking together on a balcony overlooking the river: Ken made a delicious rice and noodle stir-fry with some local mushrooms, while I steamed a fish and served it with a salsa verde made with local herbs (see page 138 for my recipe).

A multitude of plants grow well in Yunnan, and contribute to the local economy, among them tobacco, coffee and rubber. Flowers are a major crop too, some for the export cut-flower trade, but many are also used as food: day-lilies, chrysanthemums, squash flowers and jasmine buds are but a few of the many that are eaten in various ways. But perhaps the province's most famous product is tea, particularly the renowned pu-er tea.

We went into the countryside to pick tea with two local girls (from the Bulang tribe, which came from Laos and Burma centuries ago). They taught me to pick only the top bud and top two leaves from the stem. The tea is then dry-fried in a wok, rolled up and left in the sun. The leaves can be used straight away (for unfermented, 'rough' tea, which tastes good but is a little bitter), or left to ferment further (for a mature tea that tastes almost sweet). The leaves are sold loose, or in compressed shapes such as 'bricks'. The age of the bush affects the taste of the tea as well – the older the better and the more expensive: some bushes are more than 500 years old – as does the type of soil and exposure to sunlight. Many pu-er teas are sold labelled with the year of production. The whole process is almost as complex as wine-making!

The girls and I also cooked with the tea: they made a delicious salad with raw leaves and wild flowers; I stir-fried some raw leaves with chicken, and made a tea omelette for a local monk. The two girls and I, despite not speaking the same language, got on so well that we cried when it was time for us to leave. I gave them each a lipstick as a souvenir.

FISH AND SEAFOOD

SICHUAN SEA BASS with chives

I love combining meat and fish – as used in many Chinese dishes – but this meat and fish pairing is made more delicious by adding strong Sichuan flavours. Sea bass fillets are first shallow-fried in oil and then 'wokked' with a fragrant spiced oil of Sichuan chillies, Sichuan peppercorns and smoky bacon lardons, then seasoned with chilli bean paste, black rice vinegar and chilli oil – all tossed with delicious Chinese chives. This is a spicy, salty, numbing, rich dish that is full of flavour and best served with jasmine rice and iced cold beer.

Serves 2–4 to share

a pinch each of sea salt and freshly ground white pepper
1 tablespoon cornflour
400g (14oz) sea bass fillets
vegetable oil
2 small dried Sichuan chillies
¼ teaspoon Sichuan peppercorns
50g (2oz) smoked bacon lardons
1 teaspoon chilli bean paste
150g (5oz) Chinese chives (garlic chives, or baby leeks)
1 tablespoon vegetable stock (or water)
1 teaspoon Chinese black rice vinegar (or balsamic vinegar)
1 tablespoon chilli oil (see page 264)

Put the salt, white pepper and cornflour into a bowl. Add the sea bass and toss well to coat the fish in the mixture.

Fill a wok to quarter full with vegetable oil and heat the oil to 180°C/350°F, or until a cube of bread turns golden brown in 15 seconds. Lower the fish pieces into the wok and swirl in the hot oil (the Chinese call this 'passing it through the oil') for 1 minute. Pour the fish into a strainer over a heatproof bowl.

Return 1 tablespoon of the oil to the wok and reheat. (The remaining oil can be reused for another fish dish at a later date.) Add the dried chillies, Sichuan peppercorns and lardons and stir-fry in the hot oil for less than 1 minute to release their flavours (the Chinese call this *baosiung* – 'explode fragrants'). Add the chilli bean paste, then tip in the Chinese chives (or baby leeks) and toss well. Add the vegetable stock (or water) to help the chives cook and keep tossing all the ingredients together. When the chives are a deep, translucent green and have wilted, return the fish fillets to the wok and toss together, being careful not to break up the fish. Season with the vinegar and a drizzle of chilli oil, transfer to a serving plate and serve immediately, with jasmine rice.

CHING'S STEAMED SEA BREAM
with a Vietnamese mint and
wild coriander salsa verde

For our last night in Yunnan, Ken and I cooked together. Inspired by my time with the Dai minority ladies (see page 133), I thought I would simply steam a local fish in honour of the wonderful time I had spent with them fishing. And inspired by their love of the local herbs, I decided to make a salsa verde with Vietnamese mint and wild coriander to be poured over the fish once it was cooked. (See photograph overleaf.)

Serves 2–4 to share

1 x 675g (1½lb) whole, large sea bream, cleaned
2 large pinches of toasted and ground Chinese cardamom, star anise,
    Sichuan peppercorns (2 cardamoms, 3 star anise, 1 tablespoon peppercorns)
2 large pinches of sea salt

For the salsa verde
1 garlic clove, peeled, crushed and finely chopped
2.5cm (1in) piece fresh root ginger, peeled and finely chopped
8 small fresh chillies, finely sliced
2 spring onions, finely sliced
a large handful of Vietnamese mint (or a few leaves of fresh basil),
    finely chopped
a large handful of wild coriander (or farmed coriander), finely chopped
5–6 tablespoons groundnut oil
¼ teaspoon sea salt
2–3 tablespoons light soy sauce

Season the fish with the toasted Chinese spices, then season with salt on both sides. Place the fish on a heatproof plate in a bamboo steamer. Half-fill the wok with boiling water, place the steamer over the wok (making sure the base doesn't touch the water), cover and steam on high heat for 10–15 minutes until the flesh of the fish turns opaque and flakes when poked.

While the fish is cooking, combine all the salsa verde ingredients in a bowl and mix well.

To serve, pour the sauce over the fish and accompany with rice and vegetables.

FRIED FISH SNACK from Kashgar market

This tasty, crispy snack was inspired by my visit to the street market of the ancient quarters of Kashgar. I was surprised to learn that river fish are abundant here. The fish was a different culinary offering amidst all the lamb kebabs, which seem to dominate the street foods on the dusty streets of Kashgar. This is a simple but delicious quick dish.

Serves 4

450g (1lb) white firm fish fillets, such as cod, sea bass or halibut
1 teaspoon salt
cornflour, for dusting
150ml (¼ pint) groundnut or peanut oil

For the seasoning
2 tablespoons cumin powder
2 teaspoons salt
1 teaspoon freshly ground white pepper
2 teaspoons sugar

Sprinkle the fish fillets evenly on both sides with the salt. Cut the fish into strips 2.5cm (1in) wide and let these sit for 20 minutes. Then dust them with the cornflour.

Heat a wok or large frying pan over high heat until it is hot. Add the oil, and when it is very hot and slightly smoking, shallow-fry the fish strips until they are firm and cooked. Remove them with a slotted spoon and drain on kitchen paper.

Quickly mix the cumin, salt, pepper and sugar in a small bowl, then sprinkle on the crispy fish and serve at once.

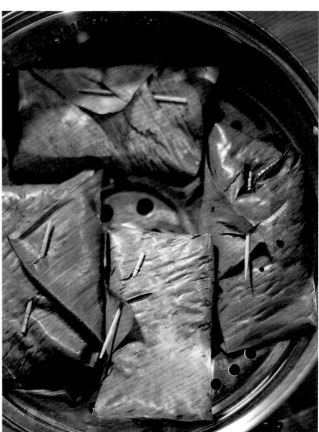

FISH IN WINE SAUCE

Fish dishes in northern China are often paired with rice wine, which gives them a rich taste. In this recipe, the fish is 'velveted', which means that it is coated with egg white, cornflour, salt and sesame oil and then gently stirred in warm, but not hot, oil. This prevents the flesh from seizing up and keeps it moist and tender. The final finish of the sauce results in a delicate and elegant dish. Serve this with plain rice for a quick and easy family meal.

Serves 2–4

50g (2oz) Chinese dried black mushrooms, pre-soaked in warm water
 for about 20 minutes until soft and pliable, then drained
450g (1lb) boneless and skinless fillets of cod, halibut, sea bass,
 or any firm white-fleshed fish, cut into 5cm (2in) pieces
150ml (¼ pint) groundnut or vegetable oil

For the coating
1 egg white (or 2 tablespoons egg white)
2 teaspoons cornflour
1 teaspoon sesame oil
½ teaspoon salt

For the sauce
3 tablespoons Shaoxing rice wine (or dry sherry)
2 teaspoons salt
freshly ground white pepper
2 teaspoons sugar
150ml (¼ pint) chicken stock
1 teaspoon cornflour, mixed with 1 teaspoon water

For the garnish
chopped spring onions

Squeeze the excess water out of the mushrooms, then cut off and discard the woody stems and finely shred the caps.

Combine the fish with all the coating ingredients in a medium-sized bowl. Mix well, then refrigerate for about 20 minutes.

Heat a wok or large frying pan over high heat until it is hot. Add the oil, and when it is just warm, quickly add the fish and stir to separate, then turn off the heat. Allow the fish to sit in the warm oil for about 2 minutes. Drain in a colander set inside a stainless steel bowl.

Reheat the wok or pan and add all the sauce ingredients, then bring to a simmer. Add the mushrooms and cook for about 2 minutes. Return the fish pieces to the pan and heat through. Serve at once garnished with spring onions.

Xi Hu Cu Yu

Sweet and sour West Lake steamed carp

I first tried this dish when I visited Hangzhou in China years ago and I loved the simplicity of it. Traditionally, carp is used for this dish but you could use sea bass or sea bream. The fish is dressed with Shaoxing rice wine, then slathered in grated ginger and steamed. While it's steaming, a delicious sauce using black rice vinegar and sugar is cooked in the wok to create a dark, rich, sweet and sour sauce, which is then poured over the cooked fish. Classic and tasty!

Serves 2-4 to share

1kg (2¼lb) fresh whole carp (or use common bream or sea bass),
   scaled and gutted
sea salt and freshly ground white pepper
2 tablespoons freshly grated root ginger
2 tablespoons Shaoxing rice wine (or dry sherry)

For the sauce
1 tablespoon groundnut oil
2 tablespoons freshly grated root ginger
1 teaspoon dark soy sauce
3 tablespoons Chinese black rice vinegar (or balsamic vinegar)
2 tablespoons soft brown sugar
125ml (4fl oz) vegetable stock
1 tablespoon cornflour, blended with 2 tablespoons cold water

For the garnish
2 spring onions, sliced into long strips, then dipped in iced water and drained,
   to make curls

Slice some slits into the side of the fish. Season with salt and white pepper on both sides and in its cavity, then rub the grated ginger all over the fish. Place on a heatproof plate that fits inside a large bamboo steamer with at least a 2.5cm (1in) margin between the plate and the steamer, then pour the rice wine (or sherry) over the fish.

Half-fill the wok with boiling water, place the steamer over the wok (making sure the base doesn't touch the water), then cover and steam for 20–25 minutes until the flesh flakes when poked with a pair of chopsticks. Turn the heat off and keep the carp warm in the steamer.

To make the sauce, heat another wok and add the groundnut oil. Add the ginger and stir-fry for a few seconds. Add the soy sauce, vinegar, sugar and vegetable stock and bring to the boil, then stir in the blended cornflour to thicken the sauce. Remove the fish from the steamer, pour the sauce over it and garnish with spring onion curls.

LONG JING CHAO XIA
Stir-fried prawns with green tea

This is perhaps one of the most famous dishes of Hangzhou. The prized *Long Jing* (Dragon Well) tea is paired with fresh live river shrimp. Legend has it that an Imperial chef mistakenly dropped some tea leaves into his wok while stir-frying white shrimp for the Emperor. Thus a classic dish was born. Many connoisseurs of Chinese tea regard *Long Jing* to be among the finest. The leaves of this green tea are prepared in a complex process that avoids fermentation. The best-quality leaves are picked before the spring rains fall, around the beginning of April when the young stems have but one tender sprout. These fragile sprouts are the basis for the tea's delicate fragrance and refreshing taste. This is an unusual, surprising combination that is distinctively exquisite, and pure and fresh at the same time.

Serves 4–6

450g (1lb) raw tiger prawns, peeled
2 teaspoons salt
1 tablespoon *Long Jing* (Dragon Well) Tea (or any Chinese green tea)
225ml (8fl oz) boiling water
1½ tablespoons groundnut or vegetable oil
1 tablespoon Shaoxing rice wine (or dry sherry)
salt and freshly ground black pepper

Devein the prawns by making a shallow cut along the back of each, then remove and discard the black vein. Rinse them well under cold running water and pat thoroughly dry with kitchen paper. Rub the prawns evenly with salt and set aside.

Put the tea leaves into a heatproof measuring jug, pour in the boiling water and leave to steep for 15 minutes.

Heat a wok over high heat until it is hot. Add the oil, and when it is hot, add the prawns and rice wine (or sherry) and stir-fry for 30 seconds. Pour in the tea and half of the tea leaves and cook for another minute. Using a slotted spoon, transfer the prawns to a serving platter. Reduce any liquid in the wok by half. Pour this over the prawns, season well with salt and pepper to taste and serve at once.

DOFU CASSEROLE

Dofu (or tofu as it is known in the West) is often misunderstood outside Asia. Invented in China and made with soya beans and then turned into curds, it comes in numerous forms: pressed in soy sauce, dried, fresh firm, fresh soft and fried. Its versatility, as well as its rich nutritional value, is what makes it so popular throughout Asia. The sponge-like texture absorbs flavours of the food it is cooked with, giving the dofu a delicate taste. This is a light and colourful dish that is perfect for the family table.

Serves 4

225g (8oz) fresh soft or silken dofu (tofu), cut into 2.5cm (1in) cubes
600ml (1 pint) chicken or vegetable stock
2 tablespoons light soy sauce
3 tablespoons Hoisin sauce
2 tablespoons whole yellow bean sauce
225g (8oz) Chinese leaves (or white cabbage), cut into 2.5cm (1in) hunks
225g (8oz) spinach, leaves only, washed
450g (1lb) raw tiger prawns, peeled and deveined (see page 147)
1 tablespoon finely chopped fresh coriander
salt and freshly ground black pepper
1 tablespoon sesame oil

Drain the dofu on kitchen paper.

Put the stock, soy sauce, Hoisin sauce and yellow bean sauce into a large, cast-iron enamel pot or Chinese clay pot and bring to the boil. Next, add the Chinese leaves (or cabbage) and boil over high heat for 2 minutes. Add the dofu, spinach and prawns, lower the heat and simmer gently for 2 minutes. Stir in the fresh coriander and season with salt and pepper. Finally, stir in the sesame oil and serve.

PHOENIX TAIL PRAWNS

This is a dish found along the eastern seacoast of China; it is called 'phoenix tail' because the butterflied prawns resemble the fanned tail of the phoenix. Instead of serving it with plum sauce, as is normal, I have made a lychee and pineapple sweet chilli jam as a dipping sauce to go with it. Be particularly careful when deep-frying in a wok.

Serves 2-4 to share

2 eggs, beaten
100g (4oz) cornflour
1–2 tablespoons water
sea salt and freshly ground white pepper
vegetable oil, for deep-frying
12 large tiger prawns, shelled, head off,
   deveined (see page 147) and butterflied
   (see right). Leave the tails on for added
   effect, if you like.

For the lychee and pineapple sweet chilli jam
50ml (2fl oz) water
50ml (2fl oz) lychee juice
50ml (2fl oz) pineapple juice
6 tablespoons granulated sugar
2 medium fresh red chillies, (de-seeded, if you like)
   roughly chopped
20g (¾oz) stoned lychees
20g (¾oz) pineapple

To butterfly prawns

Using a sharp knife, make a deep cut down the belly (underside) of the prawn (but not all the way through), then open the prawn out and press flat. Once cooked, the prawns will curl up.

First make the sweet chilli jam. Bring the water, juices and sugar to the boil, then stir to dissolve. Add the fresh chillies, lychees and pineapple and boil for about 3 minutes. Pour into a blender and blitz. Transfer to a dipping bowl and set aside – the sauce will become thick and jammy once cooled.

While the sauce is cooling, put the eggs and cornflour into a bowl and mix to a rough batter (do not mix until smooth) – you might need a little water, depending on the size of the eggs. Season with salt and white pepper.

Fill a wok less than half full with vegetable oil and heat the oil to 180°C/350°F, or until a cube of bread turns golden brown in 15 seconds. Dip each prawn in the batter, then lower into the oil and fry for 1–2 minutes until golden and the tails of the prawns have turned pink (if you've left them on). Using a slotted spoon, lift out and drain on kitchen paper. Transfer to a serving plate and serve with the sweet chilli jam.

CHEF YU BO'S FISH-FRAGRANT PRAWNS

Cooking with renowned Sichuan chef Yu Bo has been one of the highlights of my trip to China. He helped dispel the myth regarding the 'fish-fragrant' taste profile of Sichuan cooking. Traditionally, this term is used to describe a delicious sauce that has an intense fish-stock-like flavour, but it doesn't contain fish. Chef Yu Bo told us that the real explanation is that the pickled chillies that are used to make this dish were once pickled with small river fish to give the chillies a fishy flavour. He doesn't use this age-old method any more, but he does pickle his own chillies in earthenware pots. He de-seeds large cayenne-like chillies, pickles them in white liquor (*bai jiou*), salt and sugar and then grinds them into a paste. He cooks the chilli paste with a lot of vegetable oil and then adds to this spiced fragrant oil a large cup of minced garlic and ginger. It is then ready to use in this dish, which is his modern interpretation of fish-fragrant prawns – delicious! (For a vegetarian version, use fried aubergine batons instead of prawns – they work just as well.)

Makes 4

vegetable oil
4 large tiger prawns, shelled, deveined and butterflied (see pages 147 and 150),
    (or 1 large aubergine, sliced into finger-size batons)
cornflour

For the sweet and sour *yu siang* sauce
3 teaspoons icing sugar
1 tablespoon Chinese black rice vinegar (or balsamic vinegar)
1 tablespoon light soy sauce
3 tablespoons minced pickled chilli paste (Chinese supermarkets sell this)
freshly chopped chives
1 tablespoon wasabi peas, fried and crushed (optional)

To make the sauce, combine the sugar, vinegar and soy sauce in a bowl, then add the pickled chilli paste. Mix well, then add the chives and stir together. (Chef Yu Bo adds 1 tablespoon of fried baby crispy peas at this stage and tosses again – you could try using crushed fried wasabi peas.) Set to one side.

Fill a wok to quarter full with vegetable oil and heat to 180°C/350°F, or until a cube of bread turns golden brown in 10 seconds. Dip each prawn into cornflour and turn to coat, then fry for less than 2 minutes until golden brown. Drain the prawns on kitchen paper.

Spoon a teaspoonful of the sauce onto each fried prawn, transfer to a serving plate and eat immediately.

STEAMED SCALLOPS
from Huangsha seafood market

The Huangsha seafood market in Guangzhou is one of the liveliest I have ever seen in China. The streets are filled with jumping live prawns, twitching crabs, writhing sand worms, live fish swimming in tanks, even turtles and, yes, crocodiles. There is nothing fresher anywhere. I found fresh scallops and I immediately sensed that steaming was the best way to cook them. Why? Because steaming would reveal all their sweetness and freshness, and highlight their subtle taste: a perfect and most healthy way to enjoy the best harvest from the sea.

Serves 4

450g (1lb) fresh scallops, out of the shell

For the sauce
1 tablespoon finely chopped fresh ginger
1 tablespoon Shaoxing rice wine (or dry sherry)
2 tablespoons light soy sauce
1 large fresh mild red chilli, de-seeded and chopped
3 tablespoons finely shredded spring onions
3 tablespoons groundnut or vegetable oil

For the garnish
fresh coriander sprigs

Put the scallops on a heatproof plate. Next, set up a steamer or put a rack into a wok or deep pan and fill it with 5cm (2in) of water. Bring the water to the boil over a high heat. Put the scallops into the steamer or onto the rack. Turn the heat to low, cover the wok or pan tightly and steam gently for 5 minutes.

Meanwhile, combine all the sauce ingredients except the oil in a heatproof bowl. Heat a wok or large frying pan over high heat until it is hot. Add the oil, and when it is very hot and slightly smoking, pour it over the sauce ingredients.

Remove the scallops from the steamer and give the sauce several good stirs. Pour the sauce over the scallops, garnish with the fresh coriander and serve at once.

STIR-FRIED CRAB

with ginger and spring onions

Perhaps one of the greatest gifts given to me by my mother and Chinese uncles was the appreciation of fresh seafood, especially crab. Of course, at home, the crabs were always live until dispatched to the hot wok. I remember the silky texture and sweetness of the crab meat as I sucked each morsel clean. There were only ever stacks of empty shells left at the end of the meal. The Cantonese chefs know that preparing subtle and delicate food such as crab requires the minimum of seasonings: ginger, garlic and spring onions, which complement rather than detract from the crab. Eat this with friends as a first course, with your hands and perhaps a pint of beer too!

Serves 4–6

1.5–1.75kg (3–4lb) fresh or freshly cooked crab in the shell
2 tablespoons groundnut or vegetable oil
3 tablespoons finely sliced garlic
2–3 tablespoons finely shredded fresh ginger
6 whole spring onions, sliced
salt and freshly ground black pepper
3 tablespoons Shaoxing rice wine (or dry sherry)

If the crab is uncooked, put it on its back. With a thick towel, immediately twist off the large claws. Then twist off the small legs. Scrub the shells under cold running water. Now separate the top shell from the crab body. Remove the feathery lungs, the mouth and the tail. Scrub the shell and the crab body under cold running water. Remove the stomach sac. Quarter the crab body with a large knife or cleaver. Then crack the claws and legs with the flat of the cleaver. If you are using a cooked crab, simply clean and quarter the crab and crack it as described above.

Heat a wok over high heat until it is hot. Swirl in the oil, and when it is very hot and slightly smoking, toss in the garlic, ginger and spring onions and stir-fry for 20 seconds. Then chuck in the crab pieces, salt, pepper and rice wine (or sherry) and stir-fry over a high heat for about 15 minutes.

Turn out on to a large, warm serving platter and serve at once.

SMOKY HOT SCALLOPS
with bamboo shoots
and spring onions

I love scallops cooked quickly in the wok. The seasonings of soy, vinegar and brown sugar caramelise and impart a delicious smoky, sweet flavour as the edges of the scallops sear in the hot wok. A super-healthy, quick stir-fry.

Serves 2-4 to share

2 tablespoons vegetable oil
a pinch of sea salt
1 tablespoon freshly grated root ginger
2 small dried chillies
8 scallops, cleaned and corals removed (optional)
75g (3oz) shredded cooked bamboo shoots,
    sliced on the diagonal into 0.5cm (¼in) strips
2 small spring onions,
    sliced on the diagonal into 0.5cm (¼in) strips
a pinch of brown sugar
1 tablespoon light soy sauce
1 tablespoon Chinese black rice vinegar
    (or balsamic vinegar)
a dash of toasted sesame oil
1 teaspoon cornflour, blended with 1 tablespoon
    cold water

To serve
bamboo leaves, soaked and washed

Heat a wok over high heat, then add 1 tablespoon of the vegetable oil. Add the salt, ginger and chillies and toss for few seconds.

Add the scallops and toss in the wok for 1 minute, then spoon out. Add another tablespoon of vegetable oil to the wok and reheat. Add the bamboo shoots and spring onions and cook for another minute. Return the scallop mixture to the wok, then stir in the sugar and season with the soy sauce, vinegar, sesame oil and blended cornflour. Toss well. Line plates with bamboo leaves, then divide the mixture between the plates and serve immediately, with jasmine rice.

SICHUAN PROVINCE
and Chengdu City

THE CHINESE HEARTLAND OF SICHUAN

I last visited the capital city of Sichuan province, Chengdu, over 20 years ago, and when we filmed there at the beginning of 2012, Chengdu had changed beyond my wildest expectations. It is as if I went back to the future. New suburbs were mushrooming and the twisting, narrow alleys of the old city had been bulldozed to be replaced by corporate, concrete skyscrapers, all in the name of progress. One of my primary memories of Chengdu is of eating an amazing variety of street food – but in a bid to 'civilise' the city, many of the vendors have recently been encouraged to 'disappear'. However, we discovered that the food in general is better than ever, with great ingredients and dedicated, skilful chefs who are passionate about food. I could see why Sichuan cooking is taking China – and the world – by storm.

Sichuan lies in the southwest of China, and is one of the larger and more populous inland provinces (it's about the size of France). Because of its soil fertility, climate and abundance of water, Sichuan was once a major agricultural power, dubbed the country 'of heaven'. That celestial nature, however, was always countered by a poetic caveat, 'the road to Sichuan is as hard as the road to heaven'. The central plains are encircled by mountains and the huge Tibetan plain to the west, so the area was once fairly inaccessible and thus cut off from, and unfamiliar to, the rest of the country. However, a gradual process of immigration swelled the population and brought the province to national attention – as did, later, the Chengdu to Chongqing railway, the first to be built by the new People's Republic of China, in 1952. The area began to look outwards, and flourish agriculturally and socially, until the Great Famine of 1958–61: during this time some 11 million people are thought to have died in Sichuan alone. And as if this were not enough, a massive earthquake in 2008 caused a catastrophic loss of life, homes and farmland (and giant panda habitat).

However, the Chinese are very resilient, and Sichuan has regained its equilibrium in a very short space of time. Growing and producing food is still a major industry, both commercially and privately, the latter visibly demonstrated by festoons of chillies, cabbage, radish, wild mushrooms and citrus peel drying on the eaves and balconies of houses all over the province. And eating Sichuan food, for locals and visitors, is still one of the major delights of life!

Sichuan's unusual cuisine is sometimes attributed to its former geographical isolation, but the climate has probably more to do with it. The omnipresent humidity, and lack of sun, even in hot summers, means that the Chinese medicine principles of yin (cool) and yang (hot) are out of balance – the yang is particularly impaired by dampness – which can lead to ill health. The answer is to introduce a spicy heat to the food and, until the

arrival of chillies (only some 300 or so years ago), this was provided primarily by a native berry, the fruit of a prickly ash tree, known as Sichuan peppercorn or 'flower pepper' because, split, it looks like a flower bud opening. The taste is sharp, slightly spicy, but not hot, and makes the lips numb and tingly: this is known as 'ma' in Chinese, the same word that is used for 'pins and needles' and 'anaesthesia'. (Sichuan peppercorns are also one of the five spices of the famous Chinese spice mixture.) I like it, it tastes a little citrussy to me – and I love the effect it has on food.

Sichuan cuisine is famed for its bold, compound flavours and for its fiery-hot spiciness (known as *la*), pungency and fragrance: sometimes the *ma* and *la* flavourings are combined as in *ma la* rabbit. Street and restaurant foods can be both 'spicy hot' and 'numbing hot' – among them *dan dan* noodles, *mapo dofu* (see pages 106–109), *gong bao* (or *kung pao*) chicken and twice-cooked pork; but some equally famous Sichuan dishes – tea-smoked duck and crispy duck, for instance – are flavourful, but not fiery hot. The sauces for 'fish-fragrant' dishes are not actually made with fish, but with the ingredients that might complement fish dishes, such as mild chillies, ginger, garlic and spring onions: this is one of the many classic flavour combinations of Sichuanese cookery (see page 152). Chilli flavourings are often added to dishes in the form of a chilli bean sauce or paste, made from chillies and fermented beans (most authentically broad beans rather than soya beans). The principal techniques of the cooking style are stir-frying, steaming and dry-braising or dry-stewing – although Sichuan chefs claim to use over 50 distinct ways of cooking.

The number of flavours and flavour combinations in Sichuan cuisine is huge, not least because so many are sourced within the province itself: Sichuan produces soy sauce, fermented soya beans, chilli bean pastes, chilli paste, vinegars, pickles and salt. Salt was once a major source of revenue for China (probably traded on the Silk Road not far north), and the brine-salt mines of Sichuan's Zigong have supplied China's best salt for over 2,000 years. The easy availability of this has probably led to the Sichuan penchant for salt-preserved vegetables, which are a major thread of the cuisine.

Yet another thread – which in fact you find all over China – is the snack culture, *xiao chi* or 'small eats'. The Chinese love snacks probably because they breakfast lightly and thus are hungry for food long before the main midday meal. The norm of two main meals a day can often extend to at least five, due to the intervening 'small eats' meals. And, even though many of the street vendors have disappeared in Chengdu, small eats are still available, many of them from 'fly' restaurants (yes, literally fly-ridden, but often serving magnificent food) or from teahouses. Chengdu, recently dubbed the most relaxed and laid-back city in China, has more teahouses than other large Chinese cities. Every street corner boasts one, with bamboo chairs and wooden tables inside and out, where locals go to drink jasmine and other teas, to chat, socialise, pass time, eat some *xiao chi* or play *mahjong*. As an old Chengdu saying goes, referring to the dull weather of much of the Sichuan year, 'Sunny days are rare, but teahouses are abundant'!

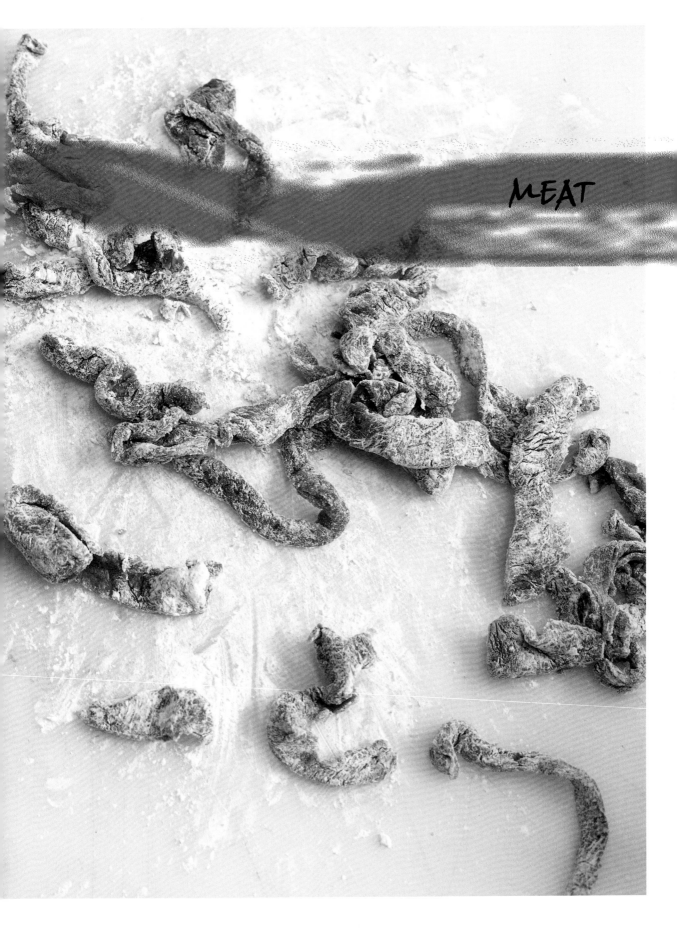

MEAT

DONGPO PORK

Legend has it that a famous official from Hangzhou, Su DongPo, was sent pork by his grateful people. Being a righteous official, he decided to share his bounty with all the workers. He instructed his cooks to cook the pork and distribute rice wine as well. Instead, the cooks mistakenly cooked the pork together with the wine, creating this classic dish. There are perhaps as many DongPo recipes as there are chefs in China, each having his or her own version. So, here is mine, which I hope would make Su DongPo and his workers very happy. This is a wonderful autumn or winter dish that can be made ahead of time and it reheats very well.

Serves 6

1.5kg (3lb) boneless pork belly, cut into 7.5 x 7.5cm (3 x 3in) pieces

For the braising liquid
6 x 7.5cm x 5mm (3 x ¼in) slices of fresh ginger
6 spring onions, cut into 7.5cm x 5mm (3 x ¼in) slices
1.2 litres (2 pints) chicken stock
600ml (1 pint) Shaoxing rice wine (or dry sherry)
3 tablespoons chilli-fermented dofu (tofu)
3 tablespoons crushed yellow bean paste or sauce
3 tablespoons Hoisin sauce
150g (5oz) Chinese rock sugar (or plain sugar)
3 whole star anise
2 pieces of Chinese cinnamon bark or sticks
2 teaspoons freshly ground white pepper
3 tablespoons whole yellow bean sauce

Fill a large pot with water and bring to a boil. Add the pork pieces and blanch for 5 minutes. Remove and drain in a colander, then quickly rinse with cold water. Discard the blanching liquid.

Put all the braising liquid ingredients into a large pot or casserole and bring to a simmer, then add the blanched pork. Cover the pot and simmer slowly for 2–2½ hours, or until the pork is very tender.

When the pork is cooked, remove it from the pot and let it cool slightly. (If you're not using it as below, the braising sauce liquid can now be cooled and frozen for re-use. Remove any surface fat before transferring it to the freezer.)

Serve the pork, like the Chinese do, in large chunks. I like to reduce the braising liquid to concentrate its flavour and then reheat the pork in it. Or you can thicken the braising liquid with a little cornflour and serve as a sauce over the sliced pork. If you do this, be sure to remove all traces of fat from the sauce before thickening it.

SWEET AND SOUR
SPARERIBS

SWEET AND SOUR SPARERIBS

This is another fabled dish in classic Chinese cookery. However, it relies on the magic of Chinese black vinegar, which is well worth the search. It has a sweet, sour and undefinable taste that gives these spareribs their reputation.

Much of the work can be done beforehand and the dish can easily be reheated. What more can you ask for? It makes a delicious main course. Be particularly careful when deep-frying in a wok.

Serves 4

750g (1½lb) pork spareribs
600ml (1 pint) groundnut or peanut oil

For the marinade
2 tablespoons Shaoxing rice wine (or dry sherry)
2 tablespoons light soy sauce
1 tablespoon Chinese black rice vinegar (or balsamic vinegar)
1 tablespoon sesame oil
salt and freshly ground black pepper
1½ tablespoons cornflour

For the sauce
1 tablespoon chopped orange zest (or a piece of Chinese dried orange peel)
3 tablespoons coarsely chopped garlic
2 teaspoons Chinese five-spice powder
3 tablespoons finely chopped spring onions
25g (1oz) Chinese rock sugar (or brown sugar)
3 tablespoons Shaoxing rice wine (or dry sherry)
150ml (¼ pint) chicken stock
1½ tablespoons light soy sauce
85ml (3fl oz) Chinese black rice vinegar (or balsamic vinegar)

Have your butcher separate the spareribs into individual ribs, and then cut into chunks about 7.5cm (3in) long. Alternatively, do this yourself using a heavy, sharp cleaver that can cut through the bones.

Mix all the marinade ingredients together in a bowl and steep the spareribs in the marinade for about 25 minutes at room temperature. Using a slotted spoon, remove the spareribs from the marinade.

Heat the oil in a deep-fat fryer or large wok. When the oil is very hot and slightly smoking, slowly brown the marinated spareribs in several batches. Drain each cooked batch on kitchen paper.

If you are using the Chinese dried orange peel, soak it in warm water for 15 minutes until it is soft, then drain and chop it coarsely. Put the chopped zest or peel together with the rest of the sauce ingredients into a clean wok or medium-sized pot. Bring the sauce to the boil, then turn the heat down, add the spareribs, cover the pan and simmer slowly for about 40 minutes, stirring occasionally. If necessary, add a little water to the sauce to prevent it from drying up. Skim off any surface fat, turn out on to a serving plate and serve at once.

LA-ROU (SMOKED PORK)
with chillies and sweetcorn

In China, *la-rou* is found in butchers or on market stalls. Smoky and delicious, it's great in stir-fries. I substitute smoked bacon lardons for the smoked pork, which are just as tasty. This simple stir-fry makes a great accompaniment to other dishes, served with rice.

Serves 2–4 to share

1 tablespoon groundnut oil
2 Sichuan dried chillies
1 medium fresh red chilli, de-seeded and finely chopped
200g (7oz) smoked bacon lardons
200g (7oz) fresh, frozen or tinned and drained sweetcorn kernels
1–2 tablespoons Chinese black rice vinegar (or balsamic vinegar)
1 tablespoon chilli oil (see page 264)
sea salt and freshly ground white pepper

Heat a wok over high heat and add the groundnut oil. Add the dried chillies, fresh chilli and bacon lardons and stir-fry for a few minutes. Add the sweetcorn and toss together. (If using fresh kernels, add a few tablespoons of water to help create some steam to cook the kernels, but let all the water evaporate before seasoning.) Season with the vinegar, chilli oil, salt and white pepper. Transfer to a serving plate and serve immediately.

STIR-FRIED PORK
with fermented dofu

Here is a classic dish that most Chinese would make at home. It is simple, easy and requires few ingredients, but its secret ingredient is fermented dofu (tofu), which has been defined as having the fifth 'umami' taste. Chinese cooks for thousands of years have realised the magic of fermented flavours, which are able to transform the most ordinary dishes into something extraordinarily delicious.

Serves 4

450g (1lb) boneless pork fillet, cut into thick slices, 5cm (2in) long
1 tablespoon Shaoxing rice wine (or dry sherry)
1 tablespoon light soy sauce
2 teaspoons sesame oil
1 teaspoon cornflour
1 tablespoon groundnut or peanut oil

For the dofu
2 teaspoons groundnut or peanut oil
8 spring onions, cut on the diagonal into 5cm (2in) lengths
3 tablespoons fermented dofu (tofu)
salt and freshly ground black pepper
2 tablespoons Shaoxing rice wine (or dry sherry)
1 teaspoon sugar

Put the sliced pork into a bowl and mix in the rice wine (or sherry), soy sauce, sesame oil and cornflour. Let the mixture sit for 10–15 minutes to allow the pork to absorb the flavours of the marinade.

Heat a wok or frying pan to a very high heat. Add 1 tablespoon of the oil, and when it is very hot and slightly smoking, add the pork slices and stir-fry until they are brown. Remove the pork from the wok and drain in a colander.

Wipe the wok clean with kitchen paper and reheat over high heat. When the wok is hot, add the 2 teaspoons of oil, then add the spring onions and stir-fry for 30 seconds. Now add the fermented dofu, smashing it against the bottom and side of the wok. Add salt and pepper to taste, the rice wine (or sherry) and, finally, the sugar. Return the drained pork to the wok and coat each piece with the sauce. Stir-fry for another 2 minutes, or until the pork is cooked through. Serve at once.

TWICE-COOKED PORK

This was quite an experience! I cooked at an organic pig farm in Pujiang with farmer Mr Peng. He invited me to cook on his farm with his wife, who prepared a traditional Sichuan feast using all parts of the pig. We cooked the classic *hui guo rou* (twice-cooked pork) together. Mr Peng suggested I use the front shoulder cut of meat. However, the piece he provided had almost 7.5cm (3in) fat before you got to the lean meat. As I was slicing it, he accused me of incorrectly cutting the meat, saying there should be slices of fat and lean meat! Had I sliced it the way he recommended, the slices of pork would have contained a huge amount of fat and then the meat would have been too large to be recognised as *hui guo rou*. So after much debate, his wife said that the best cut of meat to use for this traditional dish is pork belly – *wu hua rou*: five layers of heaven – skin, fat, meat, fat, meat. After all that debate, pork belly is supposed to be the best cut for this dish – I wish I had been told that at the beginning. The discussion was quite challenging, but it shows the passion that Sichuan people have for their cuisine.

Serves 4 to share

> 700ml (1¼ pints) water
> 300g (11oz) fatty pork belly, skin on
> 2 tablespoons groundnut oil
> 1 tablespoon Shaoxing rice wine (or dry sherry)
> 1 tablespoon chilli bean paste
> 1 tablespoon yellow bean sauce
> 1 tablespoon fermented black beans, rinsed and crushed
> 1 spring onion (or baby leek), sliced on the diagonal
>   into julienne strips (optional)
> 1 teaspoon dark soy sauce
> 1 teaspoon light soy sauce
> a pinch of sugar
> sea salt and freshly ground white pepper

Pour the water into a large pan, add the pork and bring to the boil, then boil for 30 minutes. Drain and leave to cool.

Put the meat in the fridge for about 1 hour, to firm up, then cut finely into very thin slices, about 0.5cm (¼in) thick.

Heat a wok over high heat and add the groundnut oil, then add the pork. As the pork starts to brown, add the rice wine (or sherry) and cook until the pork is browned and the skin is slightly crisp. Add the chilli bean paste, yellow bean sauce and fermented black beans and stir-fry for 1 minute.

Add the spring onion (or leek), if using, and stir-fry for less than 1 minute until well mixed. Add both soy sauces and the sugar, season and serve.

STUFFED BITTER MELON
with black bean sauce

This unusual vegetable is very much an acquired taste. It has as many detractors as it has fans, even among the Chinese, but those who love it insist it is worth the effort to appreciate its taste. Bitter melon has a bumpy dark to pale green skin, and a slightly bitter quinine flavour that has a cooling effect in one's mouth. I am among the Chinese who love it. My mother used to make it stuffed, as in this recipe. It is southern Chinese home cooking at its best.

Serves 4

750g (1½lb) bitter melons (or cucumber), unpeeled, cut into 2.5cm (1in) slices
2 tablespoons cornflour
3 tablespoons groundnut or vegetable oil

For the stuffing mixture
225g (8oz) minced fatty pork
1 egg white
1½ tablespoons finely chopped spring onions
1 tablespoon finely chopped fresh ginger
2 teaspoons Shaoxing rice wine (or dry sherry)
2 teaspoons light soy sauce
2 teaspoons sugar
1 teaspoon salt
1 teaspoon freshly ground black pepper
1 teaspoon sesame oil

For the sauce
300ml (½ pint) chicken stock
2 tablespoons Shaoxing rice wine (or dry sherry)
2 tablespoons fermented black beans, rinsed and chopped
2 tablespoons chopped garlic
2 tablespoons finely chopped fresh ginger
1 tablespoon light soy sauce
1 tablespoon oyster sauce
2 teaspoons sugar
freshly ground black pepper
1 teaspoon cornflour, mixed with 2 teaspoons water

For the garnish
2 teaspoons sesame oil
2 tablespoons finely chopped fresh coriander

Using a small sharp knife, remove the seeds and pulp from the centre of each bitter melon (or cucumber) slice. Hollow the bitter melon so that you have at least a 5mm (¼in) shell. Lightly dust the hollow interior of the slices with a little cornflour.

Mix all the stuffing ingredients together in a large bowl, then stuff each melon ring with this mixture.

Heat a wok or large frying pan until hot. Add the oil, and when it is moderately hot, add the stuffed rings and cook them slowly until they are slightly browned.

Turn them over and brown the other side, adding more oil if necessary. You may have to do this in several batches. When the rings are brown, remove them from the oil and put them on a plate. When you have fried all the rings, wipe the wok or pan clean with kitchen paper and reheat.

Mix all the sauce ingredients and put them into the reheated wok or pan. Bring the liquid to a simmer, then add the stuffed rings, cover the pan with a lid and simmer slowly for 7 minutes, or until the rings are completely cooked. Using a slotted spoon, transfer them to a serving platter.

Reduce the sauce by a third over high heat, then add the sesame oil and coriander. Pour the sauce over the stuffed bitter melons and serve at once.

YING TAO ROU Cherry pork

Mrs Peng (see page 176) showed me how to make this delicious dish. It is called *Ying tao rou*, or cherry pork, because the flavour of the liquid the pork is cooked in – an unctuous red-brown sugar syrup – is described as being as sweet as cherries.

Serves 4 to share

300g (11oz) red rock sugar (or 300ml/½ pint rich honey)
2 tablespoons vegetable oil
1 large piece pork belly (about 500g/1lb 2oz), boiled for 30 minutes, then cooled
    and sliced into 2.5cm (1in) pieces
2 tablespoons dark soy sauce
1 litre (1¾ pints) boiling water

Place the red rock sugar in a pan with about 1 litre (1¾ pints) water and cook over a high heat until reduced to a red-brown caramel syrup.

Heat a wok over high heat and add the vegetable oil. Add the pork pieces, dark soy sauce and red rock sugar syrup (or honey) and stir-fry on medium heat for 1 minute, or until coloured and browned, stirring constantly so that the sugar does not caramelise. Pour in the boiling water, cover the wok and simmer for 2 hours on medium heat, or until the pork is tender.

Serve with jasmine rice or other vegetable dishes.

CHING'S MALA CRISPY SICHUAN SAUSAGE with pickled chillies and wood ear mushrooms

At the home of our friend Jenny's aunt and grandparents in Guanghan town, Chengdu, I made a dish using her delicious *xiang chang* – Chinese sausages made from minced pork belly, *bai jiou* (white liquor), salt, sugar and chillies, which she had air-dried herself. She had been preparing them since Christmas and they were already two months old. In winter it sometimes takes one week for them to dry, but if the weather is too humid, it takes at least ten days.

      This is how my grandmother used to prepare Chinese sausage in Taiwan – fried in a wok until crispy and served with raw garlic slices.

Serves 2–4 to share

- 2 spicy Sichuan wind-dried sausages (or *lap cheong*, Cantonese dried sausage)
- a small handful of Chinese dried wood ear mushrooms, soaked in hot water for 20 minutes until soft and pliable, then drained
- 2 pickled long chillies
- 2 tablespoons vegetable oil
- 1 small bunch of Chinese garlic chives (or baby spring onions), inner stems sliced on the diagonal into 4cm (1½in) pieces
- 1 teaspoon chilli bean paste
- 1 teaspoon Sichuan peppercorns
- 1 tablespoon Sichuan pepper oil (see page 264)
- 1 tablespoon black rice vinegar (or balsamic vinegar)
- 1 tablespoon light soy sauce
- a pinch of sugar

Place the sausages in boiling water and cook for 15 minutes, then drain. Slice the sausages on the diagonal into 1cm (½in) slices. Slice the wood ear mushrooms and pickled chillies on the diagonal to resemble the long oval shape of the sausage pieces.

Heat a wok over high heat and add 1 tablespoon of the vegetable oil. Add the wood ear mushrooms, garlic chives (or spring onions) and picked chillies and toss together in the oil. Stir-fry for less than 1 minute on high heat, then spoon out onto a plate.

Place the wok back on high heat and add the remaining vegetable oil. Add the chilli bean paste, Sichuan peppercorns, Sichuan pepper oil, vinegar, light soy sauce and sugar.

Return the sausages, wood ear mushrooms, pickled chillies and garlic chives to the wok and toss together a few times in the fragrant hot oil to combine all the flavours. Take off the heat, spoon out onto a serving plate and eat immediately.

This is home comfort food at its best. With a few ingredients, my mother used to put this dish together when she came home from work. Steaming the custard gave it a smooth, velvety texture like a wonderful savoury flan. I ate it with gusto with my bowl of rice. It is a perfect, quick and inexpensive meal for just two or can be served with a stir-fried vegetable for a family lunch or dinner.

SAVOURY STEAMED EGG CUSTARD

Serves 2–4

50g (2oz) Chinese dried black mushrooms, pre-soaked in warm water
     for about 20 minutes until soft and pliable, then drained
1½ tablespoons groundnut or vegetable oil
350g (12oz) minced pork
3 tablespoons finely chopped spring onions
1½ tablespoons Shaoxing rice wine (or dry sherry)
2 teaspoons sesame oil
2 tablespoons light soy sauce
1 teaspoon sugar
1 teaspoon salt
½ teaspoon freshly ground white pepper
groundnut or vegetable oil

For the custard
4 eggs
600ml (1 pint) chicken stock
1 teaspoon salt

To serve
2 tablespoons oyster sauce

Squeeze the excess water out of the mushrooms, then cut off and discard the woody stems and finely chop the caps.

Heat a wok or large frying pan over high heat until it is hot. Add the oil, and when it is very hot and slightly smoking, add the pork and stir-fry for 2 minutes. Drain the pork, then return it to the wok. Add the spring onions, rice wine (or sherry), sesame oil, soy sauce, sugar, salt, pepper and mushrooms and continue to stir-fry for 3 minutes. Remove from the heat and set aside.

Mix all the custard ingredients in a bowl. Rub a shallow, heatproof bowl with groundnut or vegetable oil, then pour in the custard mixture.

Next, set up a steamer, or put a rack into a wok or deep pan, and fill it with 5cm (2in) of water. Bring the water to the boil over high heat. Carefully lower the bowl into the steamer or on to the rack. Turn the heat to low and cover the wok or pan tightly. Steam gently for 10–12 minutes, or until the custard has set. Add the stir-fried meat mixture and spread it over the top of the custard. Cover and steam for another 4 minutes.

Remove the bowl from the steamer, drizzle with oyster sauce and serve at once.

BRAISED DOFU with crispy pork

Qing Ming is one of the most auspicious holidays in the Chinese calendar. This is the day we visit our ancestral graves to sweep them clean and bring offerings of food. Being pragmatic, we usually bring the food home later. Traditionally, we go to the local deli and buy cooked chicken or suckling pig, or a piece of roast pork belly. When I visited my ancestral village after the offering, I cooked a typical home-style dish with a roasted pig. I braised the pork belly with dofu (tofu) in a hearty dish that exemplifies southern Chinese cooking at its best. Roast crispy pork belly can be usually found at Chinese grocers.

Serves 4

450g (1lb) fresh dofu (tofu), cut into 2.5cm (1in) cubes
    and drained in a colander for 30 minutes
450ml (¾ pint) groundnut or vegetable oil, plus 1½ tablespoons
2 tablespoons coarsely chopped garlic
2 teaspoons finely chopped fresh ginger
50g (2oz) spring onions, cut into 2.5cm (1in) strips
2 tablespoons Shaoxing rice wine (or dry sherry)
700g (1½lb) shop-bought crispy roast pork belly, boned,
    if you like, and cut into 5cm (2in) chunks
3 tablespoons oyster sauce
salt and freshly ground black pepper
50ml (2fl oz) chicken stock

For the garnish
3 tablespoons finely chopped spring onions

Prepare the dofu and leave to drain.

Heat the 450ml (¾ pint) oil in a wok until it is hot, then deep-fry the dofu (tofu) in two batches. When each batch is lightly browned, remove and drain well on kitchen paper. Let the cooking oil cool and then discard it.

Heat a wok or large frying pan over high heat, and when it is very hot and slightly smoking, add the 1½ tablespoons oil and then add the garlic, ginger and spring onions. Stir-fry for a few seconds, then add the rice wine (or sherry) and stir-fry for 30 seconds. Add the pork and dofu and stir-fry for 2 minutes.

Add the oyster sauce, salt, pepper and chicken stock. Reduce the heat to low, cover the wok and slowly simmer the mixture for 8 minutes. Turn up the heat and cook until most of the liquid has evaporated – about 1 minute. Garnish with the spring onions and serve.

Meat

CHING'S MAPO DOFU BEEF
with edamame beans

This is one of Sichuan's most famous dishes and is named after an elderly woman called Old Mrs Chen – the 'mapo' was used to describe her pockmarked complexion. She was a great cook and this dish is served in restaurants worldwide. The classic version uses *sian-miao* – thin Chinese leeks – but spring onions are a good substitute and I also like to add edamame beans (soya beans), for added texture and nutrition to round out a perfect one-pot supper dish to serve with rice. See pages 106–109 for our vegetarian versions.

Serves 4 to share

2 tablespoons groundnut oil
2 garlic cloves, peeled, crushed and finely chopped
1 tablespoon freshly grated root ginger
1 medium fresh red chilli, de-seeded and finely chopped
2 teaspoons toasted Sichuan peppercorns, ground in a pestle and mortar
300g (11oz) minced beef
1 tablespoon Shaoxing rice wine (or dry sherry)
2 tablespoons chilli bean paste
400g (14oz) fresh extra-firm dofu (tofu), cut into 2.5cm (1in) chunks
75g (3oz) fresh or frozen edamame beans
200ml (7fl oz) hot beef stock
1 tablespoon light soy sauce
1 tablespoon cornflour, blended with 2 tablespoons cold water
sea salt and freshly ground white pepper
2 large spring onions, sliced on the diagonal

Heat a wok over high heat. Add the groundnut oil, then add the garlic, ginger and fresh chilli and stir-fry for a few seconds. Add the ground peppercorns and minced beef and toss together well. As the beef starts to turn brown, add the rice wine (or sherry) and mix well, then season with the chilli bean paste. Add the dofu, edamame beans and hot stock and bring to a bubble, then mix well, being careful not to break up the dofu. Season with the soy sauce to taste, then stir in the blended cornflour to thicken the sauce and season with salt and white pepper. Garnish with spring onions and serve immediately, with jasmine or egg-fried rice.

BRAISED BEEF SHANK in Sichuan dressing

This is one of those dishes where beef shank, a cheap cut of meat that is full of muscle, is transformed into an elegant, tasty dish. I cook it slowly for hours until tender in a rich braising liquid. Once cooked, it is left to cool and then sliced, dressed and garnished. This makes a great cold starter, perfect for entertaining as it can be made hours ahead.

Serves 2-4 to share

300g (11oz) piece of braising beef (shank or shin)

For the braising sauce
500ml (17fl oz) water
2.5cm (1in) piece fresh root ginger, peeled and sliced
2 tablespoons Shaoxing rice wine (or dry sherry)
1 teaspoon Chinese five-spice powder
1 teaspoon Sichuan peppercorns
3 pieces of dried tangerine peel
1 tablespoon dark soy sauce
3 tablespoons light soy sauce
20g (¾oz) Chinese rock sugar (or 2 tablespoons soft brown sugar)
3 teaspoons caster sugar
½ teaspoon sea salt

For the Sichuan dressing
2 tablespoons chilli oil (see page 264)
¼ teaspoon toasted and ground Sichuan peppercorns
1 tablespoon Chinese clear (plain) rice vinegar (or cider vinegar)
2 tablespoons braising liquid
1 tablespoon toasted sesame oil

For the garnish
toasted white sesame seeds
1 spring onion, finely chopped

Slicing along the grain, cut the beef into four rectangular chunks. Blanch it in a pan of boiling water for 2 minutes and remove any scum. Rinse the beef, place it in a pot with all the ingredients for the braising sauce and bring to the boil. Reduce the heat, cover the pan and simmer on a low heat for 3 hours until the beef is tender and juicy. Remove and leave to cool, then keep refrigerated until ready to serve. Set aside 2 tablespoons of the braising liquid for the dressing. (You can combine the remainder with stock to make a delicious broth for soup noodles.)

Combine all the ingredients for the Sichuan dressing in a bowl and put to one side.

To serve, shred the beef and place on a serving plate. Drizzle with the Sichuan dressing, then sprinkle some toasted sesame seeds and spring onion on top and serve immediately.

STIR-FRIED BEEF

with Sichuan preserved vegetables

Beef was rarely found on my childhood dining table. My mother considered it too heavy and expensive. Instead, we had chicken, pork and plenty of vegetables. Although today I rarely eat beef, I delight in its taste when I do, especially when it's stir-fried. In this dish, I used Sichuan preserved vegetables, which have a crunchy, delicious texture and give the dish an added quality. I think you will find, as I do, that this dish is perfect for an everyday family meal.

Serves 4

450g (1lb) lean beef fillet, cut into medium thick slices, 4cm (1½in) long
2 teaspoons light soy sauce
2 teaspoons Shaoxing rice wine (or dry sherry)
1 teaspoon sesame oil
2 teaspoons cornflour
175g (6oz) Sichuan preserved vegetables, soaked for 20 minutes, then drained
1½ tablespoons groundnut or peanut oil, plus 2 teaspoons
3 tablespoons finely shredded fresh ginger
2 tablespoons chicken stock or water
salt and freshly ground white pepper
2 teaspoons Chinese black rice vinegar (or balsamic vinegar)
2 teaspoons sugar
2 teaspoons sesame oil

Put the beef slices into a bowl and add the soy sauce, rice wine (or sherry), sesame oil and cornflour. Mix well and set aside for 20 minutes. Meanwhile, rinse the preserved vegetables in several changes of water, then shred them finely.

Heat a wok or large frying pan over high heat until it is very hot. Add the 1½ tablespoons of oil, and when it is very hot and slightly smoking, add the beef and stir-fry for about 2 minutes, or until lightly browned. Drain at once into a colander over a heatproof bowl and set aside.

Clean the wok with kitchen paper and reheat it over high heat. Add the 2 teaspoons of oil, and when it is very hot and slightly smoking, stir-fry the ginger for a few seconds, then add the shredded preserved vegetables and stir-fry for another 2 minutes. Add the stock or water, salt, pepper, vinegar and sugar. Quickly return the beef to the wok to reheat and stir well. Drizzle with sesame oil, turn the mixture out on to a platter and serve at once.

HUNAN-STYLE CRISPY CHILLI BEEF
with dried chillies and peanuts

Hunan, in the south central part of China, is famous for spicy hot food and one of my favourite dishes that I had there was dry, shredded beef. Inspired by this, I created this crispy chilli beef dish, which is sweet, spicy and zesty, and delicious served with shredded lettuce and cucumber. Be particularly careful when deep-frying in a wok.

Serves 2–4 to share

450g (1lb) sirloin steak, fat removed, finely sliced into matchstick strips
3 tablespoons cornflour
groundnut oil
sea salt
4 long, dried Sichuan chillies
1 tablespoon light soy sauce
2 tablespoons sweet chilli sauce
juice and zest of ½ large orange

To serve
1 head of romaine lettuce, shredded
½ cucumber, thinly sliced

For the garnish
2 spring onions, sliced into long strips, then placed in iced water and drained, to make curls
100g (4oz) roasted unsalted peanuts

Put the beef strips into a large bowl and add 2 tablespoons of the cornflour. Toss until the beef has absorbed the cornflour. Add the remaining cornflour and toss to coat.

Half-fill a wok with groundnut oil and heat the oil to 180°C/350°F, or until a cube of bread turns golden brown in 15 seconds. Fry the beef in two or three batches until golden – 4–5 minutes. Drain on kitchen paper and season with sea salt.

Carefully drain the oil into a heatproof container, then return 1 tablespoon of oil to the wok. Heat the wok over high heat and add the dried chillies, soy sauce, chilli sauce and orange juice. Bring to a simmer and reduce the sauce until it becomes thickened and coats the back of a spoon. Toss the beef in the sauce to coat thoroughly.

Serve over a bed of the shredded lettuce and sliced cucumber, then garnish with spring onions, peanuts and orange zest.

CHINA Meat

190

BRAISED LAMB

I grew up in a very southern Cantonese, chauvinistic family, who disdained lamb, probably because they remembered it as the strong-flavoured mutton or goat eaten in China. As a result, I never experienced the taste of lamb until my mid-20s. Although I never quite acquired the taste for lamb, I grew to appreciate it more, especially when it was braised with strong aromatics and spices, as in this recipe. This dish makes a wonderful main course for autumn or winter and tastes even better made one day ahead. The bonus is that it reheats easily.

Serves 4-6

700g (1½lb) boned shoulder of lamb, cut into 5cm (2in) cubes
2 tablespoons groundnut or vegetable oil
4 whole spring onions, sliced on a slight diagonal into 7.5cm (3in) pieces
4 slices of fresh ginger
1 onion, finely chopped

For the braising sauce
1.4 litres (2½ pints) chicken stock
2 whole star anise
75g (3oz) Chinese rock sugar (or brown sugar)
2 tablespoons dark soy sauce
1 tablespoon light soy sauce
3 tablespoons Shaoxing rice wine (or dry sherry)
1 piece of Chinese cinnamon bark or cinnamon stick
3 tablespoons sesame paste (or peanut butter)
2 tablespoons Hoisin sauce
2 tablespoons yellow bean paste or sauce

For the garnish
fresh coriander sprigs

Blanch the lamb by plunging it into boiling water for 5 minutes. Then remove the meat and drain on kitchen paper, and discard the water.

Heat a wok or large frying pan over high heat until it is hot. Add the oil, and when it is very hot and slightly smoking, add the lamb cubes and stir-fry until they are brown. Add the spring onions, ginger and onion to the pan and stir-fry for 5 minutes. Transfer this mixture to a large, flameproof casserole or pot and add all the braising sauce ingredients. Bring the liquid to the boil, skim off any fat from the surface and turn the heat down as low as possible. Cover and braise for 2 hours, skimming off any surface fat from time to time.

Discard the spring onions and ginger. Arrange the cooked meat on a platter, ladle with the sauce, garnish with coriander and serve.

LIONHEAD MEATBALLS

Historical records show that this dish originated around 581–618AD when Emperor Yangdi of the Sui dynasty ordered his chefs to make a Yangzhou dish that inspired them. One of the chefs came up with a pork dish that looked so much like a lion's head that it was renamed thus. Suffice to say, it is a hearty and wonderfully rustic dish that is easy to make and equally easy to reheat. It is perfect on a cold autumn or winter evening.

Serves 4

450g (1lb) minced fatty pork
1 egg white
4 tablespoons cold water
175g (6oz) fresh or tinned water chestnuts, peeled if fresh,
    drained if tinned, and coarsely chopped
2 tablespoons light soy sauce
2 tablespoons Shaoxing rice wine (or dry sherry)
1½ tablespoons sugar
salt and freshly ground black pepper
2 teaspoons sesame oil
cornflour, for dusting
3–4 tablespoons groundnut or vegetable oil, plus 2 teaspoons
4 garlic cloves, peeled and crushed
450g (1lb) Chinese cabbage (Chinese leaves),
    stalks separated and cut into 5cm (2in) strips
450ml (¾ pint) hot chicken stock

Mix the pork with the egg white and cold water by hand. The mixture should be light and fluffy. Do not use a blender, as it would make the mixture too dense. Add the water chestnuts, soy sauce, rice wine (or sherry), sugar, salt, pepper and sesame oil and mix for another 30 seconds. Divide the mixture into six equal parts and roll each into a meatball. Dust each meatball with cornflour.

Heat a wok over high heat until it is hot. Add the 3–4 tablespoons of oil and, when it is very hot and slightly smoking, add the meatballs, turn the heat down and slowly brown them. Remove the meatballs and drain on kitchen paper.

Wipe the wok clean with kitchen paper and reheat it over high heat until it is hot. Add the remaining 2 teaspoons of oil, and when it is very hot and slightly smoking, add the garlic and stir-fry for 10 seconds. Then add the cabbage and stir-fry for 20 seconds. Add the hot stock and continue to cook for 2 minutes until the leaves are soft. Transfer the mixture to a heavy, flameproof casserole. Lay the meatballs on top of the leaves, bring the mixture to a boil, then turn the heat to very low, cover and simmer for 1½ hours.

Arrange the cabbage on a platter and lay the meatballs on top, then pour the sauce over the dish and serve at once.

YANG ROU BING

Finely shredded mutton and spring onion wheat flour pancake parcels

Mutton is eaten a lot by the Uighur Muslims throughout China. It is a strongly flavoured meat that is quite tough, so the trick to cooking it is to slice the meat very finely into very thin shreds and then stir-fry with soy, ginger and rice wine. This meaty filling is delicious stuffed into wheat flour pancakes or warmed small pitta pockets, then garnished with sesame seeds and spring onions.

Serves 2–4 to share

12 wheat flour pancakes (shop bought, or small pitta-bread pockets, cut in halves)
1 tablespoon groundnut oil
1 tablespoon freshly grated root ginger
300g (11oz) mutton, finely sliced into shreds
1 tablespoon Shaoxing rice wine (or dry sherry)
½ teaspoon dark soy sauce
1 tablespoon light soy sauce
a pinch of sugar
2 tablespoons hot vegetable stock
1 teaspoon cornflour, blended with 1 tablespoon cold water
4 spring onions, very finely chopped

For the garnish
toasted sesame seeds
a dash of toasted sesame oil

Put the wheat flour pancakes (or pitta) into a small bamboo steamer. Half-fill a small wok with boiling water, place the steamer over the wok (making sure the base doesn't touch the water), then cover and steam on medium-high heat for 5 minutes.

While the pancakes are steaming, heat another large wok and add the groundnut oil. Add the ginger and stir-fry for a few seconds. Add the mutton and break it up, then toss well. As the mutton starts to turn brown, add the rice wine (or sherry) and stir-fry for 1–2 minutes until fragrant and the mutton is cooked. Add both soy sauces, the sugar and hot stock and bring to a bubble, then stir in the blended cornflour and toss well. When the meat is glossy, toss in the spring onions. Take off the heat and transfer to a serving plate, then sprinkle with toasted sesame seeds and season with the sesame oil.

To serve, fold the pancakes in half and then in half again into a cone shape. Fill the inside with the mutton and spring onion filling and serve immediately.

STIR-FRIED LAMB WITH LEEKS

Here is my interpretation of a classic northern stir-fry lamb recipe with leeks, a member of the onion family. The sweetness of the Hoisin sauce and the spicy prick of the Sichuan peppercorns give this dish its perfect lift.

Serves 4

450g (1lb) boneless lamb fillet, cut into medium slices
1 tablespoon Shaoxing rice wine (or dry sherry)
1 tablespoon light soy sauce
2 teaspoons sesame oil
2 teaspoons cornflour
3 tablespoons groundnut or peanut oil
175g (6oz) leeks, cleaned, white part only finely shredded
    into 7.5cm (3in) lengths
6 garlic cloves, peeled and thinly sliced
1 tablespoon finely chopped fresh ginger
salt and freshly ground black pepper
2 tablespoons Hoisin sauce
1 teaspoon ground roasted Sichuan peppercorns

Put the lamb into a bowl, add the rice wine (or sherry), soy sauce, sesame oil and cornflour and set aside.

Heat a wok until it is hot. Add 2 tablespoons of the oil, and when the oil is very hot and slightly smoking, add the marinated lamb pieces and stir-fry over high heat for 2 minutes. Drain at once into a colander over a heatproof bowl and set aside.

Reheat the wok until it is hot, then add the remaining 1 tablespoon of oil. Add the shredded leeks, garlic and ginger and stir-fry for another 3 minutes. Return the lamb to the wok, add the salt, pepper and Hoisin sauce and stir-fry for another 2 minutes, or until the lamb is heated through.

Turn out on to a serving platter, sprinkle with the ground peppercorns and serve straight away.

Meat

KEN

KASHGAR

KASHGAR AND THE SILK ROAD

Neither Ken nor I had ever been this far west in China before, and the region and its principal city were strange. The people don't look remotely Chinese – more Persian or Arabic – and they spoke a dialect we didn't understand, so we had to have both a guide and a translator. The region, Xinjiang, is extreme and harsh, and Kashgar is an almost medieval oasis city, situated in a basin between high mountains and the forbidding desert of Taklamakan, which translates as 'Go in and you won't come out'.

We couldn't fly the 4,000km (2,500 miles) directly from Beijing to the city of Kashgar, and had to stop off at Urumqi en route. Kashgar has been used since ancient times by travellers on what was known as the Silk Road. This historical network of trade routes, no more than camel tracks at first, started in Xi'an (where the terracotta warriors were found). It extended over 6,000km (3,700 miles), and connected Asia with the Western world, beginning some 200 years BCE. The network got its name from the primary trade item from China – silk – but the Chinese also offered teas, jade, lacquer ware and porcelain. (A less welcome export from China along the Silk Road was the bubonic plague, which devastated Europe in the 14th century.) However, the traffic was very much two-way: China also received foreign goods, ideas – Buddhism spread from India to China along the Silk Road – and foodstuffs.

Kashgar is a Muslim city, based in the predominantly Muslim province of Xinjiang. A Turkic people, known now as the Uighurs, came to this part of Asia a millennium ago, bringing Islam with them, and displacing Buddhism. Xinjiang – the largest administrative province in China, roughly the size of Iran – has always been disputed territory, leading to much tension over the years. Many Uighurs are separatist, and believe that China's claim to their homeland is a form of imperialism; the Chinese insist that the territory has always been an integral part of the Chinese nation. The Uighurs at one time were the most numerous group in Xinjiang, but Han Chinese migrants have poured into the region, encouraged by government and attracted by new industrial towns and farming villages.

But the old city of Kashgar still stands, just, a prime example of a traditional Islamic city; it has over 100 mosques, including the Id Kah, the largest in China. In a sense, Kashgar is closer to Mecca than Beijing, especially in culinary terms, with a distinct Central Asian, even Middle Eastern, flavour. Lamb or mutton is eaten 365 days a year. It is roasted whole (in tandoor-type ovens), skewered and grilled as tender kebabs, stewed and curried, and minced as filling for a variety of little pasties or dumplings: one of them was called *samsa*, the Uighur version of samosa, perhaps? We cooked with our guide Muhammad Yusuf's family: Ken was taught how to make these mini lamb pies, and I learned how to make *laghman* – the local thick, udon-like noodles. I also helped to make a huge batch of dumplings which, strangely, looked very similar to Italian tortellini!

In Kashgar they eat noodles with mutton, local spinach and tomato in a wet, soup-like broth. (It was strange to see such un-Chinese-looking people eating out of a bowl with chopsticks in such a Chinese manner – normally they eat with their hands here.) A rice platter made with mutton or chicken, and decorated with sultanas and nuts, is known variously as *pilaf* or *plov*, or *polo*, another example of a Middle Eastern leaning.

Kashgar seasonings include saffron, cumin, raisins, apricot kernels (our guide said they were good for men's fertility), and very mild chilli: they don't like spiciness at all, and prefer their food almost bland. They drink a very sweet black tea – made with rosebuds, cinnamon, cardamom and honey – in the morning and before dinner. They also eat a lot of yoghurt, made from yak's, mare's, camel's or cow's milk, and have it throughout the meal, alongside other food, but not for dessert. We did, however, see Chinese influences too: on the streets they were offering sticky rice dumplings, made using traditional bamboo steamers, *zong-zi* dumplings (sweet, with a date in the middle), and a variety of fruits. The region claims to have the best fruit in China, especially melons, as it is very hot and dry in summer; the water for irrigation comes from glaciers in the surrounding mountains.

Bread is central to the cuisine here, and is the wheat flatbread found throughout central Asia. It is known here (as in India) as naan: huge circles of dough are stamped with intricate patterns and then baked on the sides of pot-bellied clay ovens. (The bread stamp is made from nails, or chicken feather quills, arranged in a pattern on a base.) Ken and I made bread with a local family: after stamping, the bread was smeared with a paste made from red onion, sesame seeds, salt and spices. When I slapped my bread onto the wall of the oven, it peeled off and looked terrible. Ken's was perfect! Naan is eaten with everything, all day long – even for breakfast, when they have it with yoghurt and honey. It has almost a sacred significance to the Uighur people: it must not be thrown away, and in naan's presence, lies are forbidden and vows are binding (bread plays a large part in Uighur weddings).

Kashgar has a very important Sunday market, appropriate for a city that for so many years was the first (or last) stop on the Silk Road. Thousands of people swarm into the city to sell fruit, vegetables and meat – the latter in the form of live lambs, goats, cows and chickens. Horses and donkeys, occasionally camels, are on offer as well, not for food but for farm work: a special area is set aside for prospective buyers to 'test-drive' their chosen steeds. (The area around Kashgar is not known as the Chinese Wild West for nothing!) Food stalls are everywhere, selling bread, snacks, dumplings, noodles, soup, kebabs and tea. They also sell silk and carpets as well as local craft items, such as copper teapots, wooden jewellery boxes, bread stamps, boots with turned-up toes, and hundreds of types of hats.

The region felt very alien to me, like stepping back 2,000 years in time. Culturally it was strange: for example, we went to a Chinese New Year party, where the men and the women were kept completely separate, which didn't seem very festive to me. It's not my place to comment, as it's not my culture, but it isn't how I'd like to live. The women seem happy enough, although they appeared to do all the work. It's just a different world and a different way of living.

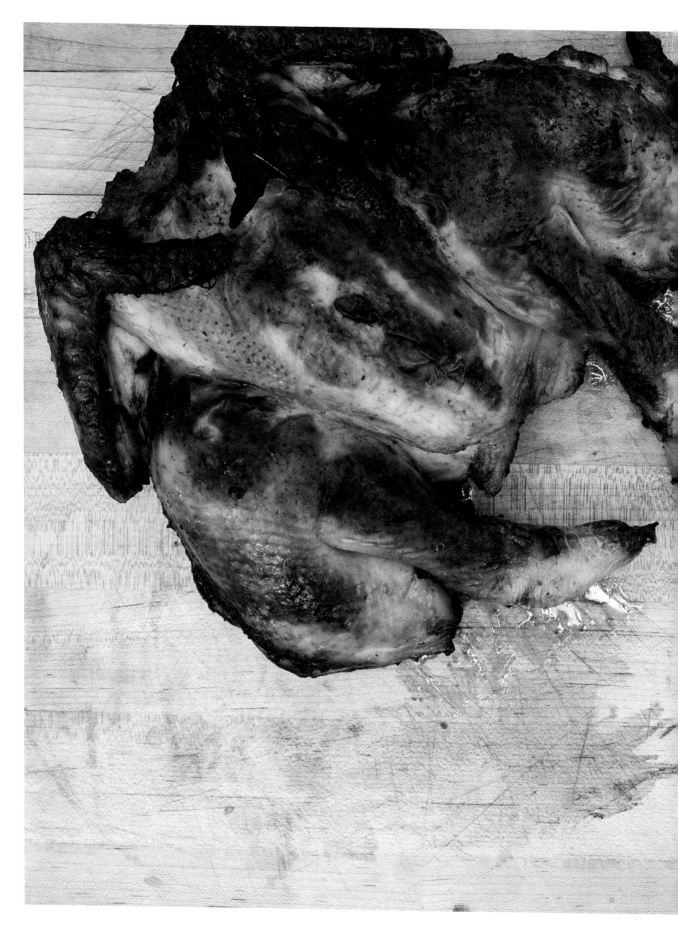

POULTRY

SICHUAN FRIED SPICY CHICKEN

with green pepper

I love spicy chicken – threads of chicken are coated in an egg white and cornflour mixture (a technique called 'velveting' where the meat retains its juiciness when shallow-fried), then stir-fried with aromatics, garlic and ginger, tossed with green pepper and seasoned with a spicy, soy, rice wine sauce. The result is rich, savoury and mouthwateringly good.

Serves 2–4 to share

1 egg white
1 tablespoon cornflour
150g (5oz) chicken thighs, skinned, boned and sliced into long, thin julienne strips
sea salt and freshly ground white pepper
vegetable oil, for shallow-frying
2 garlic cloves, peeled and minced
2.5cm (1in) piece fresh root ginger, peeled and grated
1 green pepper, de-seeded and cut into long thin matchsticks
2 large fresh cayenne chillies, de-seeded and sliced into long, thin julienne strips
1 teaspoon chilli bean paste
1 teaspoon yellow bean paste (or sweet bean paste or yellow miso)
1 tablespoon Shaoxing rice wine (or dry sherry)
1 teaspoon light soy sauce

For the garnish
1 spring onion, sliced into long strips, then dipped in iced water and drained, to make curls

Put the egg white into a bowl with the cornflour and mix well. Add the chicken strips and coat well. Season with salt and white pepper.

Fill a wok one-third full with vegetable oil and heat the oil to 180°C/350°F, or until a cube of bread turns golden brown in 15 seconds. Carefully lower the chicken pieces into the hot oil and fry for 2 minutes, or until the chicken is cooked through. Pour the chicken into a strainer over a heatproof bowl, then return 1 tablespoon of oil to the wok and reheat. Add the garlic and ginger and toss for a few seconds, then add the green pepper and fresh chillies, with a small splash of water to help create some steam to cook the vegetables, and toss through.

Return the chicken to the wok and season with the chilli bean paste, yellow bean paste (or miso), rice wine (or sherry) and soy sauce and toss together well to coat the vegetables and the chicken. Transfer to a serving plate, garnish with spring onion curls and serve immediately.

YU SIANG SHREDDED CHICKEN

and aubergine

Yu siang is otherwise known as 'fish-fragrant' and is one of the flavour profiles found in Sichuan cooking (see page 152). I like to make this dish with shreds of chicken and tender aubergines coated in a delicious sauce – perfect with plain jasmine rice.

Serves 2-4

sea salt and freshly ground white pepper
1 tablespoon cornflour
300g (11oz) chicken thighs, skinned, boned and sliced into julienne strips
3 tablespoons groundnut oil
1 tablespoon Shaoxing rice wine (or dry sherry)
1 aubergine, sliced into batons and tossed in vegetable oil
2 garlic cloves, peeled, crushed and finely chopped
2.5cm (1in) piece fresh root ginger, grated
1 fresh red cayenne chilli, de-seeded and finely chopped
1 tablespoon chilli bean paste
1 spring onion, finely sliced

For the sauce
100ml (3½fl oz) cold vegetable stock
1 tablespoon light soy sauce
1 tablespoon Chinese black rice vinegar (or balsamic vinegar)

Put the salt, white pepper and cornflour into a bowl, add the chicken pieces and toss well to coat in the mixture.

Heat a wok over high heat and add 1 tablespoon of the groundnut oil. Add the chicken pieces and toss well, then stir-fry for 1 minute. Add the rice wine (or sherry) and cook for 2 minutes, or until the chicken is cooked through, then put to one side.

Clean out the wok with kitchen paper, then heat over medium heat and add another tablespoon of groundnut oil. Add the aubergine and stir-fry until browned, then cook, stirring, for 5 minutes until softened. Keep adding small drops of water to create some steam to help soften the aubergines as it cooks. Transfer to a plate and set aside.

Place the wok back on high heat and add the remaining groundnut oil. Add the garlic, ginger, fresh chilli and chilli bean paste and cook for a few seconds. Return the cooked aubergine to the wok, followed by all the ingredients for the sauce, then tip in the chicken strips and bring to the bubble.

Cook until the sauce has thickened, then stir in the spring onion. Remove from the heat and serve immediately, with jasmine rice.

STEAMED WINED CHICKEN

with dried mushrooms, bamboo shoots, and goji berries

This nutritious dish is easy to prepare. Do try to use organic chicken where possible, as the quality of the meat will be better than non-organic and the health benefits of this dish will be greater, especially when coupled with the goji berries and dried Chinese mushrooms, which are full of antioxidants and vitamins. The bamboo shoots add texture and crunch. Serve this with plain steamed rice and stir-fried vegetables for a healthy supper.

Serves 2 or 4 to share

 1 tablespoon groundnut oil
 sea salt and freshly ground white pepper
 2 tablespoons Shaoxing rice wine (or dry sherry)
 1 tablespoon sesame oil
 4 chicken thighs, skinned, boned and sliced
 2.5cm (1in) piece fresh root ginger, peeled and sliced
 2 fresh shiitake mushrooms, sliced
 1 small tin bamboo shoots, drained
 a handful of dried goji berries

Combine the groundnut oil, salt, white pepper, rice wine (or sherry) and sesame oil in a bowl.

Toss all the remaining ingredients in the rice wine dressing. Arrange on a small, heatproof plate that fits inside a bamboo steamer. Place the steamer over a small pan of boiling water (making sure the base doesn't touch the water) and steam on high heat for 15 minutes. Check that the chicken is cooked through – insert a skewer into the meat and if the juices run clear the chicken is cooked. Serve immediately, with Stir-fried Spinach (try Ken's recipe on page 94) and jasmine rice.

CANTONESE-STYLE ROAST PI-PA CHICKEN

I love this poetic name for such a delicious chicken dish. It is named after the Chinese musical instrument called the *pi-pa*, which is similar to a lute in the West. Here the chicken is prepared very much like the French method *en crapaudine*, which means the chicken is split down the back and flattened to look like a toad. The secret to the success of the recipe is in the drying process. If you have patience, you will be rewarded with an outstanding dish. It is well worth the wait, as you will see.

Serves 4-6

1 x 1.5kg (3–3½lb) chicken

For the coating mixture
4 tablespoons clear (plain) rice vinegar (or cider vinegar)
1 tablespoon red rice vinegar
2 teaspoons Shaoxing rice wine (or dry sherry)
2 teaspoons honey
3 tablespoons water

For the marinade
1½ tablespoons Chinese rose liqueur wine (or cognac)
1 tablespoon red fermented dofu (tofu)
1 tablespoon fermented black beans, rinsed
1 teaspoon Chinese five-spice powder
1 tablespoon finely chopped garlic
2 teaspoons salt
2½ tablespoons sugar

To butterfly the chicken, split it open down the back (not through the breast side) and remove the backbone. Flatten it out with the palm of your hand, pushing against the top of the chicken. Make two small holes, one either side of the end of the breastbone, and tuck the legs through. This will hold the shape of the bird while it roasts.

Bring some water to the boil in a wok or shallow pan and blanch the chicken (skin side only) for 5 minutes. Remove the chicken from the water and allow to dry for 1 hour in a cool draughty place, or in front of a fan.

Put all the coating ingredients in a wok and bring to a boil, then coat the skin side of the chicken several times with this mixture. Allow the chicken to dry again. Once the chicken has dried, the surface of the skin should feel like parchment.

Meanwhile, place all the marinade ingredients in a blender and whizz to combine, then rub this evenly on the inside of the chicken. Place the chicken, skin side down, on a rack and leave to marinate, uncovered, in a cool, draughty place for at least 4 hours or overnight in a fridge.

Preheat the oven to 230°C/450°F/gas 8. Place the chicken, skin side up, on a baking tray and bake for 5 minutes. Lower the oven temperature to 180°C/350°F/mark 4 and continue to cook for 30–40 minutes, or until the chicken is brown and crispy.

Remove from the oven and let the chicken sit for 15 minutes, then carve into serving pieces and serve at once.

STEAMED CANTONESE-STYLE CHICKEN
with fermented dofu

Fermented dofu (tofu) is otherwise known as *dofu ru* and can be found in jars in Chinese supermarkets. It comes in many different varieties and these are known as 'Chinese cheese'. They are made from fermented soya beans and have an intensely salty, umami-rich flavour. When I was growing up, *dofu ru* was a staple food, paired with congee (rice porridge) and pickles for breakfast. These salty, moreish cubes are fantastic used in marinades for meats such as chicken and pork. I like to use them in a marinade for chicken, then steam the chicken thighs, remove the meat from the bone and serve with a dipping sauce of chilli black rice vinegar – simple and tasty - in celebration of Cantonese cooking. If you cannot find *dofu ru*, use a tablespoon of yellow bean paste.

Serves 2–4 to share

4 chicken thighs, skinned, bone in

For the marinade
2 tablespoons groundnut oil
2 garlic cloves, peeled and finely chopped
1 tablespoon freshly grated root ginger
2 tablespoons Shaoxing rice wine (or dry sherry)
1 teaspoon dark soy sauce
1 tablespoon light soy sauce
2 cubes of fermented dofu (*dofu ru,* optional)
1 cube of red fermented dofu (*dofu ru,* optional)
1 tablespoon toasted sesame oil

For the dipping sauce
2 tablespoons Chinese black rice vinegar (or balsamic vinegar)
1 medium fresh red chilli, de-seeded and finely chopped

Combine all the ingredients for the marinade, add the chicken pieces and toss to coat in the mixture, then cover and marinate in the fridge for 1 hour.

Place the chicken and marinade on a heatproof plate that fits inside a bamboo steamer. Half-fill a wok with boiling water, place the steamer over the wok (making sure the base doesn't touch the water), then cover and steam on high heat for 30 minutes.

Meanwhile, combine the vinegar and chilli for the dipping sauce and set aside.

Remove the chicken and test to see if it is cooked – insert a skewer into the meat nearest the bone and if the meat juices run clear the chicken is cooked. Remove from the steamer, then bone and cut into bite-sized pieces or shred into strips. Pour the cooking juices over the chicken and serve with the vinegar and dipping sauce.

CHING'S CHICKEN and green tea maocha

I cooked this simple, experimental but delicious dish for the two girls from the Bulang tribe I met in Yunnan (see page 133), both nicknamed Xiao-Yu, at home in their tea-picking village. The girls' grandmother gave me a freshly killed and prepared chicken and I chopped it into 2.5cm (1in) pieces. Everything except the innards was used, including the neck, head and feet. I used raw pu-er tea leaves (see below) and maocha (sun-dried rough pu-er tea) in the dish, together with some brewed pu-er maocha tea. The result is a delicious light, bittersweet chicken broth. Finally, I added some local Chinese greens (but you can use tenderstem broccoli). Surprisingly, the slight bitterness of the tea leaves enhances the sweetness of the chicken meat. This is delicious with jasmine rice.

Serves 2–4 to share

2 tablespoons vegetable oil
2 tablespoons raw green pu-er tea leaves, sliced (see page 126)
1 tablespoon cooked and sun-dried pu-er (maocha) leaves
1 x 2kg (4½lb) whole chicken, chopped into 5cm (2in) pieces on the bone
1 teaspoon salt
450ml (¾ pint) brewed maocha tea (or vegetable stock)
225ml (8fl oz) water
300g (11oz) tenderstem broccoli

Heat a wok over high heat and add the vegetable oil. Add the green pu-er tea leaves and the cooked maocha and stir-fry for less than 1 minute. Add the chicken pieces and salt and stir-fry on high heat for 10 minutes.

Add the brewed maocha tea (or stock) and cook uncovered for 10 minutes. Add the water and bring to the boil. Toss in the broccoli and stir-fry for 1 minute until tender. Spoon out and serve immediately with jasmine rice.

BRAISED FIVE-SPICE CHICKEN WINGS
with bamboo shoots

I love to cook what I love to eat. This dish combines my favourite Chinese flavours – wok-cooked chicken wings with soy sauce and five-spice, with bamboo shoots. It is an easy recipe – first marinate the chicken, then gently braise it in the wok until cooked through. The result is a tasty dish, perfect for all the family. Make sure you buy free-range or organic chicken, which is healthier and will taste better than non-organic.

Serves 2–4 to share

8 chicken wings
2 tablespoons groundnut oil
225g (8oz) tinned sliced bamboo shoots
200ml (7fl oz) hot chicken stock
1 tablespoon cornflour, blended with 2 tablespoons cold water
2 spring onions, sliced into 5cm (2in) pieces

For the marinade
2 garlic cloves, peeled and crushed
1 tablespoon freshly grated root ginger
1 teaspoon Chinese five-spice powder
3 tablespoons light soy sauce
1 teaspoon dark soy sauce
3 tablespoons Shaoxing rice wine (or dry sherry)
2 tablespoons soft brown sugar

Combine all the ingredients for the marinade in a large bowl, add the chicken wings and toss to coat in the mixture, then cover and leave to marinate in the fridge for 1 hour.

Heat a wok over high heat and add the groundnut oil. Drain the chicken, reserving the marinade, and add to the wok with the bamboo shoots. Stirring gently on medium heat, cook for 10 minutes until browned on all sides. Pour in the reserved marinade and the hot stock and braise on medium heat for 10 minutes, or until the chicken is cooked through and tender. Add the blended cornflour and stir until thickened. Add the spring onions, toss through well, then cook for 1 minute and serve immediately.

BANG-BANG CHICKEN

The name 'bang-bang' comes from the Mandarin word for 'stick', which is *bung*. The chicken meat is beaten with a stick to help tenderise it, so it shreds easily; you could use a rolling pin to flatten the cooked chicken and then use your fingers to tear it into shreds.

Serves 2

100g (4oz) vermicelli mung bean noodles (or rice noodles), pre-soaked in hot water for 5–6 minutes and drained (optional)
250g (9oz) poached chicken breast, shredded
½ cucumber, cut in half lengthways, de-seeded and sliced into long, thin julienne strips
40g (1½oz) radish, sliced
40g (1½oz) carrot, peeled and sliced into long, thin julienne strips

For the dressing
2 tablespoons groundnut oil
1 tablespoon toasted sesame oil
2 tablespoons sesame paste (or tahini blended with 1 teaspoon toasted sesame oil)
1 tablespoon crunchy peanut butter
1 tablespoon light soy sauce
1 tablespoon freshly grated root ginger
2 tablespoons Chinese black rice vinegar (or balsamic vinegar)
½ teaspoon dried chilli flakes
½ teaspoon ground Sichuan peppercorns

For the garnish
1 medium fresh red chilli, de-seeded and finely chopped
1 large spring onion, finely sliced lengthways
toasted black and white sesame seeds

Arrange the noodles, if using, on a plate. Layer the chicken, cucumber, radish and carrot on top, then chill.

Before serving, put all the ingredients for the dressing into a blender and whizz to combine. Drizzle the dressing over the dish, then sprinkle with the fresh chilli, spring onion and toasted sesame seeds. Serve immediately.

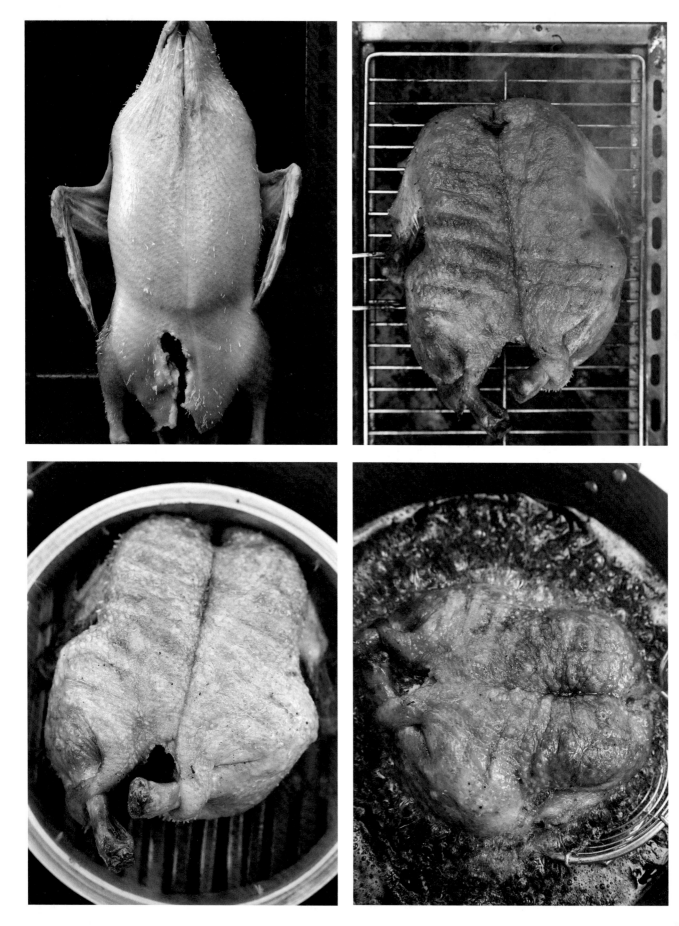

TEA-SMOKED DUCK SICHUAN-STYLE

I love duck in all its forms, whether it's roasted, braised or smoked – its rich and deep-flavoured meat is unique, and we Chinese appreciate this delicious bird. Once it is marinated, it reminds me of delectable, aged smoked ham.

    The smoking process adds a lovely, mysterious *je ne sais quoi* to the duck. Of course, frying it at the end ensures crispy skin. I love to serve it just as it is, but you can serve it with Chinese pancakes (see page 99) or steamed buns, as they do in Sichuan. When you have tasted this duck, you will understand why all the effort is worthwhile. It makes a very elegant dinner party dish for a special occasion.

    Be particularly careful when deep-frying in a wok.

Serve 4–6

1 x 1.6–1.8kg (3½–4lb) duck, fresh or frozen
50g (2oz) camphor wood chips (or hickory chips)
25g (1oz) jasmine tea leaves
750ml (1¼ pints) groundnut or vegetable oil, for deep-frying

For the marinade
5 tablespoons salt
2 tablespoons roasted and ground Sichuan peppercorns
2 tablespoons sesame oil
150ml (¼ pint) Shaoxing rice wine (or dry sherry)
600ml (1 pint) water

TEA-SMOKED DUCK SICHUAN-STYLE

continued

If the duck is frozen, thaw it thoroughly. To butterfly the duck, split it open down the back (not through the breast side) and remove the backbone. Flatten it out with the palm of your hand, pushing against the top of the duck. Make two small holes, one on either side of the end of the breastbone, and tuck the legs through. This will help hold the shape of the duck when it is marinating and later when it is smoked.

Combine the marinade ingredients in a medium-sized bowl, mixing well to dissolve the salt. Place the duck in a shallow, non-corrosive pan and pour the marinade over it. Cover with clingfilm and refrigerate for 8 hours, or overnight.

Bring some water to the boil in a wok or shallow pan and blanch the duck (skin side only) for 2 minutes. Remove the duck from the water and allow it to dry in front of a fan for at least 3 hours.

Soak the wood chips in water. Make a charcoal fire in an outdoor grill and, when the coals are ash white, add the wood chips and tea leaves. Place the duck, skin side down, on the grill, cover and leave to smoke for about 35 minutes. Remove the duck from the grill. Set up a steamer, or put a rack into a wok or deep pan, and fill it with 5cm (2in) water, then gently steam the duck for 1½ hours. Allow it to cool thoroughly. The duck can be prepared ahead to this point, but it should be thoroughly dried before frying.

Heat a wok or large, deep, flameproof casserole over high heat until it is hot, then add the oil and heat until it is very hot. Deep-fry the duck until it is golden and crispy – about 8–10 minutes. Drain well on kitchen paper, then chop up and serve.

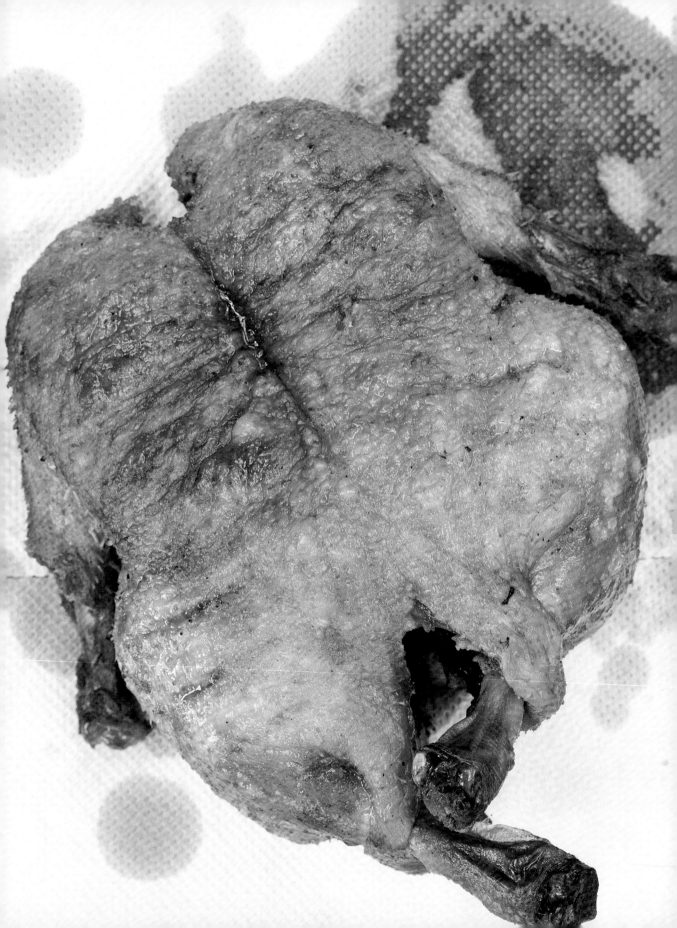

STIR-FRIED MINCED DUCK

in fresh lettuce cups

I am proud to be part of the southern Chinese heritage. We have not only been at China's forefront politically, but also economically. In our cuisine, we have readily adapted to outside influences – in this case, crispy fresh lettuce, which we would normally blanch, is used as a textural foil to the rich duck meat that has been stir-fried. It makes a delicious, satisfying and easy dish to serve to family or friends.

Serves 4

1 iceberg lettuce
1½ tablespoons groundnut or vegetable oil
finely chopped meat from thighs and legs of a cooked or smoked duck
50g (2oz) fresh or tinned water chestnuts, peeled if fresh, drained if tinned, and sliced
4 tablespoons finely chopped spring onions
1 tablespoon finely chopped fresh ginger
1 tablespoon finely chopped garlic
1 tablespoon Shaoxing rice wine (or dry sherry)
1 tablespoon oyster sauce
1 teaspoon light soy sauce
salt and freshly ground black pepper
2 teaspoons sesame oil
Hoisin sauce, for dipping

Separate the iceberg lettuce leaves into single cups. Keep refrigerated until ready to serve.

Heat a wok over high heat until it is very hot. Add the oil, and when it is very hot, add the chopped duck meat, chestnuts, spring onions, ginger and garlic and stir-fry for 2 minutes. Add the rice wine (or sherry) and the oyster and soy sauces, then salt and pepper to taste. Finally, drizzle in the sesame oil and turn on to a platter.

Arrange the lettuce leaves on a separate platter, put the Hoisin sauce into a small bowl and serve at once.

YUNNAN-STYLE ROAST DUCK

I must be biased, but I think the Chinese are the best at cooking duck. The secret is in the preparation. The hot liquid to baste the duck and seal the skin and then the long drying ensures crispy skin and moist meat.

This Yunnan duck speciality uses the same principle as Beijing (Peking) duck, with the exception of the use of honey (which is abundant in the region) and the unique combination of condiments and seasonings used as dipping sauces, but it is not served with pancakes or steamed buns. However, the result is the same ... sheer deliciousness! This makes a wonderful centrepiece for any special dinner party.

Serves 6–8

1 x 1.6–1.75kg (3½–4lb) duck, fresh or frozen
salt and freshly ground black pepper
3 tablespoons honey

For the basting liquid
1 litre (1¾ pints) water
1½ tablespoons dark soy sauce
1½ tablespoons honey
1 tablespoon clear (plain) rice vinegar (or cider vinegar)

For the dipping sauces
5 tablespoons Hoisin sauce, mixed with 2 tablespoons chilli
    bean sauce
2 tablespoons salt, mixed with 1 tablespoon roasted ground
    Sichuan peppercorns
6 spring onions, cut into 5cm (2in) segments

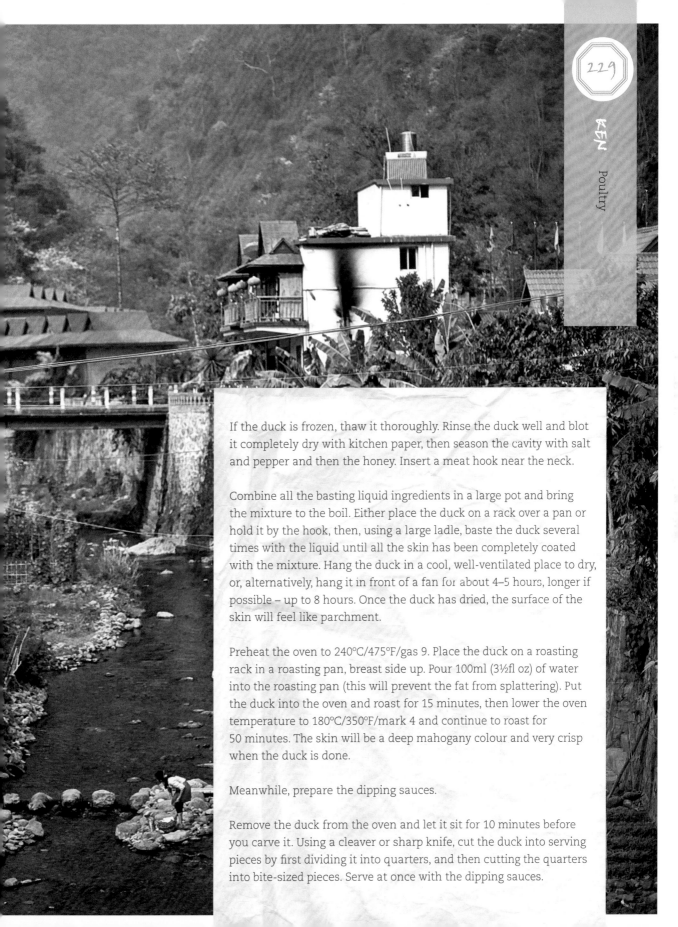

If the duck is frozen, thaw it thoroughly. Rinse the duck well and blot it completely dry with kitchen paper, then season the cavity with salt and pepper and then the honey. Insert a meat hook near the neck.

Combine all the basting liquid ingredients in a large pot and bring the mixture to the boil. Either place the duck on a rack over a pan or hold it by the hook, then, using a large ladle, baste the duck several times with the liquid until all the skin has been completely coated with the mixture. Hang the duck in a cool, well-ventilated place to dry, or, alternatively, hang it in front of a fan for about 4–5 hours, longer if possible – up to 8 hours. Once the duck has dried, the surface of the skin will feel like parchment.

Preheat the oven to 240°C/475°F/gas 9. Place the duck on a roasting rack in a roasting pan, breast side up. Pour 100ml (3½fl oz) of water into the roasting pan (this will prevent the fat from splattering). Put the duck into the oven and roast for 15 minutes, then lower the oven temperature to 180°C/350°F/mark 4 and continue to roast for 50 minutes. The skin will be a deep mahogany colour and very crisp when the duck is done.

Meanwhile, prepare the dipping sauces.

Remove the duck from the oven and let it sit for 10 minutes before you carve it. Using a cleaver or sharp knife, cut the duck into serving pieces by first dividing it into quarters, and then cutting the quarters into bite-sized pieces. Serve at once with the dipping sauces.

KEN'S PEKING DUCK

Peking duck is perhaps one of the most famous Chinese dishes. Its history goes back to the Yuan Dynasty around 1330, when it is first mentioned by an Imperial inspector in an early cook book. I suspect the technique of roasting is Mongolian in origin. The dish remained on the Imperial menu and the first Peking duck restaurant opened in Beijing around the 1500s, when the capital shifted from Nanjing to Beijing. The fame of the dish grew in time, and rightfully so.

I think it is probably one of the best techniques of roasting duck in the world. The preparation and cooking of Beijing (Peking) duck in China is an art form in itself. Specially raised ducklings are fed a rich diet of maize, sorghum, barley and soya bean for 1½ months before they are ready for the kitchen. After the ducks are killed and cleaned, air is pumped through the windpipe to separate the skin from the meat. (This allows the skin to roast separately and remain crisp, while the fat melts, keeping the meat moist.) Hot water is then poured over the duck to close the skin pores and it is hung up to dry. During the drying process, a solution of malt sugar is liberally brushed over the duck and it is then roasted in a wood-burning oven using wood from fruit trees, which gives the duck a unique fragrance. The result is a shiny, crisp and aromatic duck with beautiful brown skin, moist flesh and no fat.

Preparing Beijing (Peking) duck is a time-consuming task, but I have devised a simpler method that closely approximates the real thing. Just give yourself plenty of time and the results will be good enough for an emperor. Traditionally, Beijing (Peking) duck is served with Chinese pancakes, spring onions cut into brush shapes and sweet bean sauce. In Hong Kong and in the West Hoisin sauce is used instead (this is very similar to sweet bean sauce but contains vinegar). Each guest spoons some sauce on to a pancake. Then a helping of crisp skin and meat is placed on top, with a spring onion brush, and the entire mixture is rolled up like a stuffed pancake. It can be eaten using chopsticks or with your fingers. This makes an unforgettable dish for a very special dinner party.

If you are ambitious and want to serve a three-course Beijing (Peking) duck feast, then use some of the cooked meat for Stir-fried Minced Duck in Fresh Lettuce Cups (see page 226) as a second course and finish with Peking Duck Soup (see page 39).

KEN'S PEKING DUCK continued

Serves 4–6

1 x 1.6–1.75 kg (3½–4 lb) duck, fresh or frozen
1.2 litres (2 pints) water
150ml (¼ pint) Chinese black rice vinegar (or balsamic vinegar)
3 tablespoons malt/maltose sugar (or honey)
3 tablespoons dark soy sauce
1½ tablespoons coarse salt
2½ tablespoons Chinese five-spice powder
2 teaspoons roasted ground Sichuan peppercorns

To serve
1 recipe Chinese Pancakes (see page 99)
24 spring onions, cut into brushes (see below)
6 tablespoons Hoisin sauce (or sweet bean sauce)

If the duck is frozen, thaw it thoroughly. Rinse the duck well and blot it completely dry with kitchen paper. Insert a meat hook near the neck.

Bring the water and vinegar to the boil in a large pot. Hold the duck by the hook over the pot and, using a large ladle, carefully pour this mixture over the outside of the duck several times, as if to bathe it, until all the skin is completely coated with the mixture. Reserve the mixture. Hang the duck in a cool, well-ventilated place to dry, or alternatively hang it in front of a cold fan for about 2–3 hours, or overnight. When the duck is dried, bring the reserved water–vinegar liquid to the boil, add the sugar (or honey) and soy sauce and again bathe the duck skin and leave to dry in front of fan for at least 2–3 hours more. Once the duck has dried, the surface of the skin will feel like parchment. Mix the salt, five-spice and peppercorns together and rub this mixture evenly inside the cavity of the duck.

Preheat the oven to 240°C/475°F/gas 9. Meanwhile, place the duck on a roasting rack in a roasting pan, breast side up. Pour 150ml (¼ pint) of water into the pan (this will prevent the fat from splattering). Roast for 15 minutes, then lower the oven temperature to 180°C/350°F/gas 4 and continue to roast for 1 hour and 10 minutes.

While the duck is roasting, make the spring onion brushes. Cut off and discard the green part of the spring onion then trim off the base. You should be left with a 7.5cm (3in) white segment. Make a lengthways cut of about 2.5cm (1in) long at one end of the spring onion. Roll the spring onion 90° and cut again. Repeat this process at the other end. Soak the cut spring onions in iced water and they will curl into brushes. Pat them dry before use.

Remove the duck from the oven and let it sit for at least 10 minutes before you carve it. Using a cleaver or a sharp knife, cut the skin and meat into pieces and arrange them on a warm platter. Serve at once with Chinese pancakes, spring onion brushes and a bowl of Hoisin sauce (or sweet bean sauce).

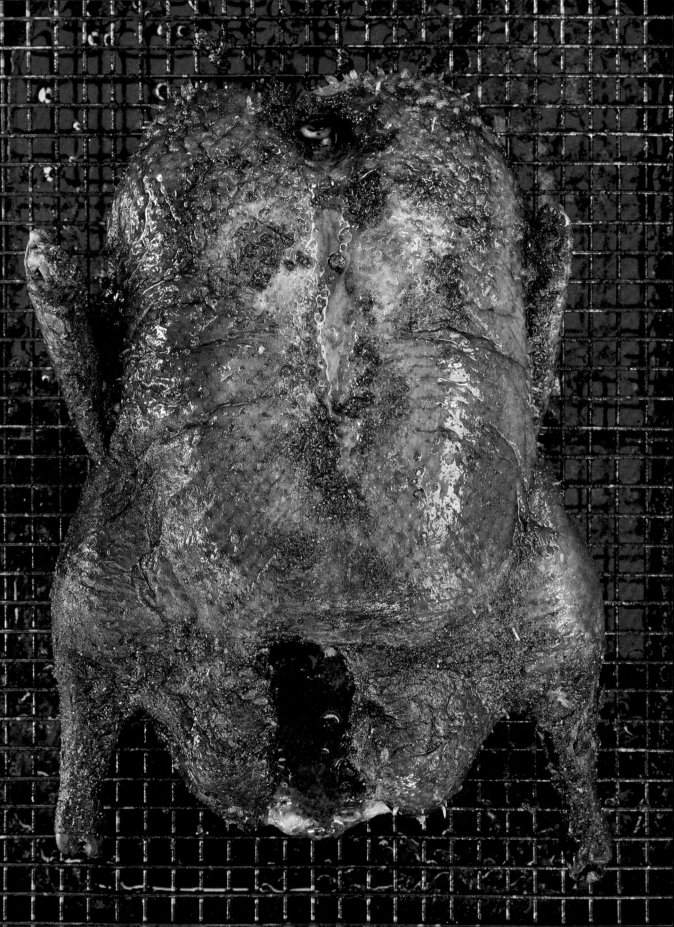

CHING'S PEKING DUCK

I love Peking duck and have been trying to perfect this recipe for many years. However, since I don't have a wood-fired oven at home, just a conventional one, the result is a cross between a roast Cantonese-style duck and Peking duck. The Cantonese influence is in the use of five-spice, ginger, star anise and shallot stuffing. I also brine the duck in a solution of brown sugar, vinegar and water. The trick, of course, is to hang the duck up to dry for several hours before roasting, and then roast for a long period of time at a consistent heat until the fat renders and the skin is really crisp. Go that one step further and fry the duck once cooked for a crispy, aromatic-style duck found in Chinese restaurants all over the world. Serve with steamed wheat flour pancakes with cucumber slices and spring onion threads. Try to find Chinese mandarin Peking ducks and not muscovy ducks, as they have less fat and, therefore, will give a crispier skin. Duck-elicious!

Serves 8 to share

3kg (6½lb) duck
150ml (¼ pint) boiling water
50g (2oz) soft brown sugar
1½ tablespoons sea salt
1 tablespoon Chinese five-spice powder
2.5cm (1in) piece fresh root ginger, peeled and grated
2 shallots, peeled and finely chopped
2 star anise
peanut oil (optional)

For the brining solution
150g (5oz) brown sugar
1 tablespoon salt
200ml (7fl oz) boiled warm water
700ml (1¼ pints) cold water
300ml (½ pint) Chinese clear (plain) rice vinegar (or cider vinegar)

To serve
24 wheat flour pancakes (shop bought)
75g (3oz) sweet bean paste (or Hoisin or plum sauce)
2 spring onions, sliced lengthways into long thin strips
1 cucumber, de-seeded and sliced into long, thin julienne strips

Clean the duck and cut off its wings, then remove the duck's innards (you can use these for stock). Wash the duck cavity well, then pat dry. Using a sharp skewer, make small pricks all over the skin, being careful not to damage the skin too much.

Hold the duck by its neck over the sink and carefully pour boiling water all over the skin to blanch and tighten it. Pat the duck dry inside and out.

To make the brining solution, dissolve the sugar and salt in the boiled warm water, then mix with the cold water and add the vinegar. Place the duck in a brining bag (or a deep bowl) and pour the brining solution over it. Place in the fridge and leave to marinate for 3 hours, turning the duck over halfway through to ensure even brining. This helps to keep the meat juicy as it cooks and give the duck a tangy flavour.

Remove the duck from the brine and pat dry. Discard the brining solution. Insert a meat hook near the neck and hang the duck in a cool dry place for 8 hours (you can set a fan over it to air-dry the duck, as this will help to make the skin crisp as it cooks).

Combine the sugar, salt and five-spice and rub this thoroughly inside the duck. Then stuff the duck with the ginger, shallots and star anise and, using a stainless steel needle, seal the opening.

When ready to cook the duck, preheat the oven to 150°C/300°F/gas mark 2. Place the duck, breast side up, on a roasting rack over a roasting tin. Cook the duck for 1¼ hours, turning the duck over halfway through to ensure even cooking. Increase the heat to 240°C/475°F/gas mark 9 and cook for 10–15 minutes more to crisp up the skin.

If you like your duck even crispier and aromatic, heat a pan of peanut oil to 180°C/350°F, or until a cube of bread turns golden brown in 15 seconds. Place the duck, on its rack, over a large hot wok and carefully ladle the hot oil over the skin to crisp it further and until the skin turns golden brown.

Place the wheat flour pancakes in a small bamboo steamer (you may have to do this in two batches) and place the steamer over a small pan of boiling water (making sure the base doesn't touch the water). Steam for 6–7 minutes, then remove the steamer from the pan. Carve the duck at the table and serve with the bean paste (or Hoisin/plum sauce), spring onions and cucumber strips. To make each pancake, dip a little duck in the sauce, place it in the centre of the pancake, place some spring onion and cucumber on top, then roll up and eat.

DA DONG'S SHREDDED DUCK

with Sichuan flavours

Da Dong is widely regarded as one of the best chefs in China today. When I met him and tasted his food I understood why he deserved this accolade. Although he is from Beijing and made one of the best versions of Peking duck I have ever tasted, his real skill is in how he has re-interpreted regional dishes garnered from his travels throughout China. In this recipe, inspired by his version, but without the shredded pig ears, cooked duck was shredded and tossed in a fragrant Sichuan-flavoured sauce. It was outstanding because of its subtle use of Sichuan spices.

Serves 4

450g (1lb) cooked duck meat from either Peking Duck or Tea-smoked Duck
(see pages 230–233 or 234–237, or 222–225)

For the sauce
1 tablespoon dark soy sauce
2 teaspoons Chinese black rice vinegar (or balsamic vinegar)
2 tablespoons chilli bean sauce
2 teaspoons sesame oil
2 teaspoons sugar
½ teaspoon roasted and ground Sichuan peppercorns
1½ tablespoons finely chopped spring onions

Shred the duck skin and meat into fine shreds.

Mix all the sauce ingredients together in a bowl. Add the duck meat and turn to coat the pieces thoroughly with the sauce, then leave it to sit for 15 minutes before serving at room temperature.

BEIJING

BEIJING: capital cuisine

My brother and his family live in Beijing, so I visit often. It is a bustling, busy, polluted city, much of it new, built around the splendours of the ancient Forbidden City. We eat at home quite a lot of the time, but we also eat out, in some of the many, and very varied, restaurants in our area. Beijing is opening up to the outside world – and it did so spectacularly during the 2008 Olympics – but it is not all to the good. Several fast-food chains have arrived in the last few years, and the Chinese are starting to like Westernised food.

I love the feel of Beijing, which is much more scholarly than other parts of China. The people are more chic and outgoing too: elsewhere people tend to keep themselves to themselves, but here they are a lot friendlier. You see people with dogs and other pets, which is unusual, and there are modern buildings, which give the city a very up-to-date, global feel. But the city also has an ancient history, keeping hold of its roots, and I like to see old and new together. This combination is reflected in the food, which has traditional Muslim and Mongolian influences as well as new ideas: there are Mexican, Italian and French-style cafés, and you can even buy churros! It's so different to how it used to be, when you could only buy noodles, dumplings and food in home-style restaurants.

Traditional Beijing or Peking cuisine – also known as Mandarin cuisine – is a culinary melting pot. At heart it is a northern cuisine, so is influenced by climate: for instance, the food staples of the region are wheat and corn rather than the rice of the warmer and rainier south (rice here is seen as a treat!). The basics of traditional Beijing eating – usually at open-air stalls and in night markets – are noodles, usually served in a broth, and eaten sometimes for breakfast, piping hot in winter, cold in summer. This is what workers, whether from construction sites or high-rise offices, will eat for lunch – if they don't choose Western... Other basic Beijing staples are wheat-flour dumplings and buns: *baozi* is a yeast-raised bun, white and pillow-like, served with a variety of fillings (*char siu*, red bean paste); *xiaolongbao* are smaller stuffed buns, their dough wrapping thinner, so they are more like dumplings; and *jiaozi* are horn-shaped dumplings.

We went to the Black Sesame kitchen cookery school in Beijing, where dumpling master Chairman Wang taught us the techniques of perfect pan-fried and water-cooked dumplings. Chairman Wang had previously been teaching at a traditional cookery school, with written exams and no practical elements. Jen Lin Liu, the owner of the school, didn't like this scholarly approach, so set up a school based on hands-on cooking, and invited Chairman Wang to join her. Much like baking in the West, making and eating dumplings brings families together (especially at Chinese New Year, when gold-ingot-shaped dumplings signify wealth).

The cuisine of Beijing has also been influenced by its neighbours' cooking styles, which range from the sophisticated dishes of Shandong and Jiangsu to the south, to the simpler cooking of Mongolia to the north. The recipe Beggar's chicken probably originated further south: a

chicken is spiced, stuffed and wrapped in lotus leaves and foil (once it would have been mud), then baked. There are many lamb and mutton dishes in restaurants, echoes of Mongolian and Muslim influence. Cabbage is a staple here, as it is in Shandong dishes, especially in winter, and the widespread use of vinegar in Beijing cooking probably owes a lot to the fact that both the nearby provinces of Shandong and Jiangsu produce wonderful vinegars.

But a primary influence on traditional Beijing cuisine was the banquet-style cooking of the Imperial Palace. Some banquets – in which ingredients like shark's fin, sea cucumber, deer tendons and fish lips would feature – would consist of over 100 courses. Peking duck – which Ken says he would like as his last supper! – comes from this Imperial tradition. We cooked Peking duck with chef Jiang Xiao at Liqun: to dry-inflate the duck before roasting, he blew with his mouth, although it is more usual nowadays to use a bamboo pipe (I have even used a bicycle pump!). The owner of the restaurant is Zhang Li Qun and his personal story is amazing. From a very poor rural background, he couldn't afford to buy the bricks needed to make a Peking duck oven, so he travelled around on his three-wheeled bike collecting bricks from old, knocked-down houses and from builder friends. He re-formed the bricks by hand and used them to build his first oven. Now his restaurant, in one of the surviving hutongs (alleys), is one of the most respected in Beijing.

We also cooked with renowned chef Zhenxing Da Dong. He uses different techniques for Peking duck, including cooking the duck for twice as long so that all the fat drips out – making a much healthier meal. What was consistent both at Liqun and with Da Dong, though, was the skill of the chefs: they instinctively knew how to treat the duck, and when to rotate it so that it was perfectly cooked and a rich golden brown all over.

Cooking in Beijing, as in the whole of China, was dealt a severe blow when Mao Zedong came to power in 1949. The years of his rule saw the deaths of millions from starvation; his nationalisation of private businesses, including restaurants, meant that no-one cooked any more, and generations-old traditions and skills went into near terminal decline. It is only in the last 20 or so years that home cooking and restaurants are flourishing again, and this is probably due to the retained memories of Beijing elders such as Chairman Wong. Their suffering during those lost years has also given them a certain discipline, which they have used to find an inner peace. Chairman Wong, although an older lady, refused to sit down when making her dumplings, and stood the whole time…

DESSERTS

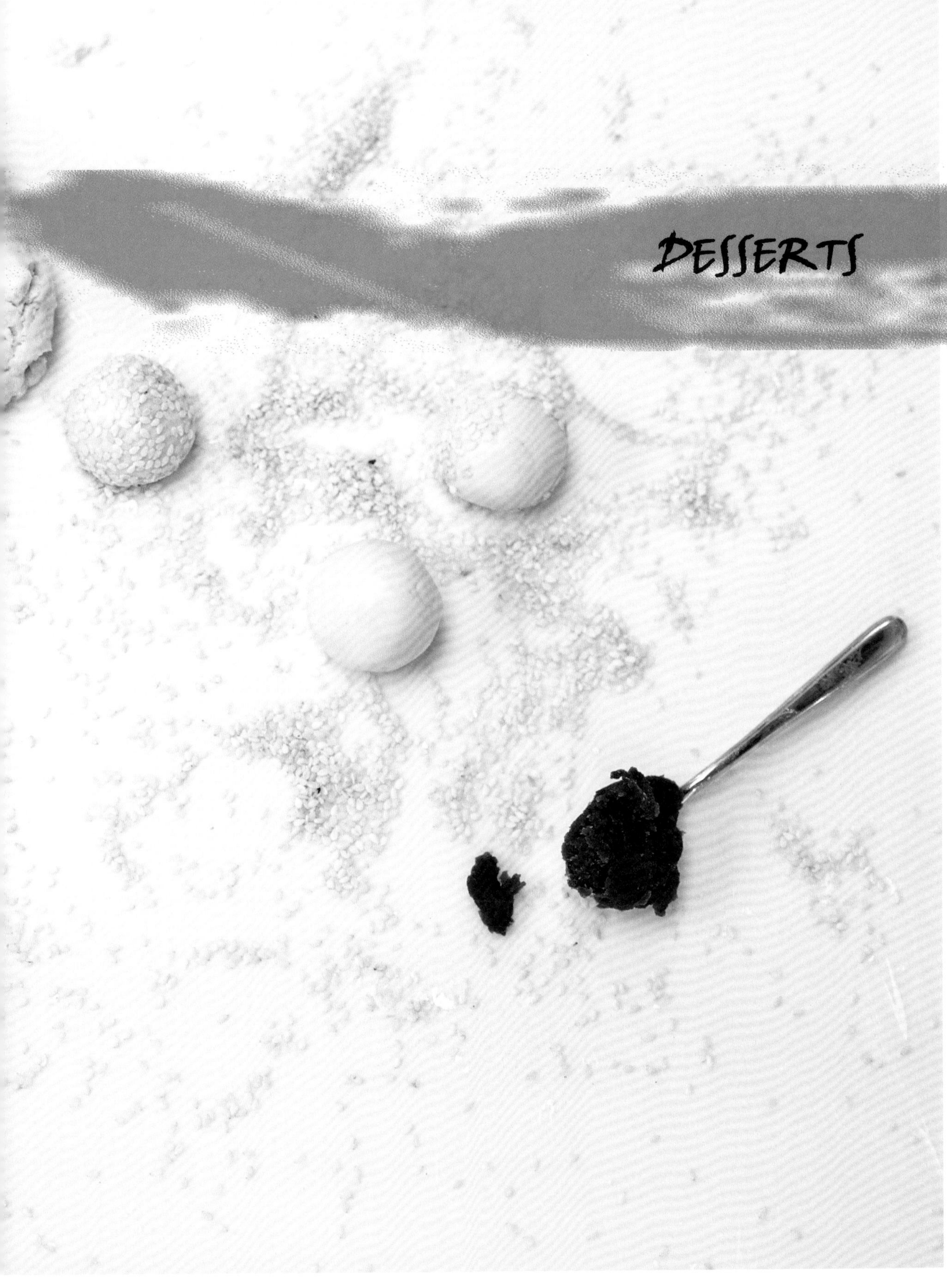

RED BEAN SESAME BALLS

Yum. Who doesn't like sesame balls? Fried, sticky, nutty balls that are like chewy doughnuts but taste even better with a sweet centre – sweet red adzuki bean paste. In fact, you could stuff them with chocolate, bananas, lotus bean paste, and so on. To ensure that the dough remains soft as you work, keep a dampened tea towel over it when not in use – this will help keep the dough malleable and allow you to fill and roll it up into balls. Glutinous rice flour dough is not the easiest to work with, but the result is worth it. When the balls are deep-fried, they turn a golden brown, puff up and float to the surface (make sure you keep the heat on medium and keep tossing the balls in the hot oil to cook the dough through) and as with any deep-frying, take care – a wok lid or spatter-proof shield works well if you have some balls that spit!

Serves 4 / makes 12 balls

250g (9oz) glutinous rice flour, plus extra for dusting
60g (2½oz) soft brown sugar, dissolved in 100ml (3½fl oz)
    boiling water in a jug
100ml (3½fl oz) cold water
100g (4oz) tinned adzuki red bean paste
75g (3oz) white sesame seeds
650ml (1 pint 2fl oz) groundnut oil, for deep-frying

Put the rice flour into a bowl and make a well in the centre. Stir the sugar and boiling water to ensure the sugar has dissolved, then pour it into the flour and add the cold water. Combine to make a dough and knead for about 5 minutes into a ball.

Dust your hands with some rice flour, then break the dough into 12 balls, roughly the size of golf balls.

Holding a dough ball in one hand, use the thumb of the other to make a hole in the dough to form a cup, with thin sides. Press 1 teaspoon of red bean paste into the middle and gather the edges of the dough together so that the paste is completely covered. Do this with all the dough, then roll each of the balls in your hands until perfectly round and roll them in the sesame seeds.

Heat the oil in a deep-fat fryer or wok to 160°C/325°F, or until a tiny piece of the dough browns in 30 seconds. Deep-fry the balls, a few at a time, until the sesame seeds turn golden brown and the balls start to float to the surface – 6–8 minutes.

Once cooked, place the sesame balls on a tray lined with kitchen paper to drain off excess oil while you cook the remainder. Serve warm.

PEACH AND LYCHEE SPRING ROLLS

I love spring rolls but find they taste even better with a sweet filling – and nothing beats fresh lychees and ripe peaches. Wrap them in bought spring roll pastry and fry until golden, then serve with ice cream and maple syrup – easy and delicious! Perfect for a summer or Chinese New Year party.

Serves 4

12 x 15cm (6in) square spring roll wrappers
10 fresh lychees, peeled, halved and stoned
   (or use tinned lychees)
2 large ripe peaches, stoned and thickly sliced
   (no need to peel)
1 tablespoon cornflour, blended with
   1 tablespoon warm water
groundnut oil, for shallow-frying

To serve
vanilla ice cream
golden syrup

Place a spring roll wrapper in front of you, in the shape of a diamond (with points top and bottom).

Put a chopped lychee and a few peach slices across the centre of the pastry, then brush each corner with the blended cornflour. Reserve the leftover lychees and peaches for decorating. Bring the two side corners over the filling to the middle. Bring the bottom corner up over the filling, then brush the remaining corner with a little more blended cornflour and roll up from the bottom to secure the spring roll. Continue in the same way until all the wrappers are filled.

Heat a large non-stick frying pan or wok over medium heat. Add a shallow layer of oil, allow to heat, then fry the spring rolls for 1 minute until golden. Turn the rolls over and cook the other side until golden.

To serve, put 2 or 3 spring rolls in each small serving dish, top with a scoop of vanilla ice cream and decorate with the leftover pieces of fruit. Drizzle with golden syrup and serve immediately.

MANGO, LYCHEE AND PASSION FRUIT SALAD with star anise sugar

Nothing beats a refreshing exotic fruit salad to end a meal. You can use any fruits you like, but I love to combine mangoes, tinned lychees and passion fruit. Dragon fruit would be just as delicious. I like to spice up the salad with some star anise sugar for a fragrant rich sweetness.

Serves 4

2 ripe mangoes, sliced into wedges
1 pineapple, peeled and sliced into wedges
1 x 425g tin lychees, drained
2 passion fruit
1 star anise
2 tablespoons white granulated sugar

For the garnish
4 fresh mint sprigs

Chill the mango, pineapple and lychees in the fridge for 1 hour.

When cold, divide between four bowls and drizzle with passion fruit pulp.

Grind the star anise in a spice grinder until you have a fine powder, then mix with the sugar and sprinkle over the fruit. Garnish each bowl with a mint sprig and serve.

CUSTARD TARTLETS
from Guangzhou Restaurant

These custard tartlets are inspired by Chef Zheng Bo, a talented *dim sum* chef, who shared with me his recipe for these popular snacks. Chef Bo's version calls for lard and butter in the pastry, but I decided to use only butter. His secret is to roll and fold the pastry three times in a row, resulting in a flaky pastry which is irresistible when filled with the light, delicate, silky custard.

Makes 8–10 tartlets

150ml (¼ pint) water
4 tablespoons caster sugar
1 tablespoon milk
3 small eggs, beaten

For the pastry
100g (4oz) plain flour, plus extra for dusting
4 tablespoons butter, cut into small pieces
2 tablespoons caster sugar
2 tablespoons double cream

Mix the ingredients for the pastry together in a bowl or in a food processor. Roll the pastry into a ball, then roll out on a lightly floured surface and fold and roll at least three times. Roll into a ball, wrap with clingfilm and refrigerate for at least 30 minutes.

Boil the water and sugar in a saucepan for 5 minutes to make a light syrup, then take off the heat and leave to cool thoroughly.

Preheat the oven to 190°C/375°F/gas mark 5.

Roll out the pastry to about 0.5cm (¼in) thick and press into small tart moulds.

Combine the cooled syrup with the milk and eggs, then divide evenly between the tart moulds.

Bake the tartlets for 10 minutes. Lower the oven temperature to 160°C/325°F/gas mark 3 and bake for a further 10 minutes, or until the custard just sets. Leave to cool before serving.

CHILLED WATERMELON
dipped in a lime and raspberry coulis

Desserts never featured much on my family's kitchen table – after a meal we ate whatever fruits were in season. I always looked forward to watermelon season, and the refreshing sweetness of the flesh was even better when slightly chilled. This has become my favourite recipe to make when entertaining friends and family – it's delicious and fun to eat, especially for children.

Serves 4

350g (12oz) raspberries
2 tablespoons maple syrup
zest and juice of 1 lime
½ watermelon, skinned and cut into 2cm (¾in) dice

For the garnish
small fresh mint leaves

Prepare the coulis by blending 250g (9oz) of the raspberries with the maple syrup, lime zest and juice. When smooth, pass through a sieve and spoon into four small dipping dishes.

Divide the watermelon cubes and remaining raspberries between four plates, garnish with the mint leaves and serve with the coulis.

VANILLA STICKY CAKE with cinnamon sugar

Traditionally, this is served at Chinese New Year. It is a sweetened dough made with glutinous rice flour. The dough is steamed and left to cool and set, then it's dipped in an egg batter and fried until the outside is golden but the inside is soft, pillowy and chewy. This is one of my favourite Chinese desserts. I like to add a touch of vanilla extract to the sweetened dough and, once the pieces have been fried golden brown, I sprinkle some cinnamon sugar on them while they're hot – they're like soft, chewy Chinese doughnuts!

Serves 2–4 to share

200ml (7fl oz) water
125g (4½oz) brown sugar
150g (5oz) glutinous rice flour
25g (1oz) wheat starch
1 teaspoon vanilla extract
groundnut oil, for deep-frying

For the batter
100g (4oz) potato flour (starch)
2 eggs, beaten
a pinch of sea salt
1–2 tablespoons cold water (if needed)

For the cinnamon sugar
2 teaspoons ground cinnamon
2 tablespoons granulated sugar

Bring the water to the boil, then stir in the brown sugar until dissolved. Leave to cool.

Sift the rice flour and wheat starch into a bowl, pour in the cooled sugar liquid and vanilla extract and mix to a silky batter consistency. Place in a thin circular tray or foil container on a heatproof plate that fits inside a bamboo steamer. Half-fill the wok with boiling water, place the steamer over the wok (making sure the base doesn't touch the water), then cover and steam on high heat for 1 hour. Check the wok occasionally and, if necessary, top up with boiling water.

Leave to cool for 30 minutes, then refrigerate until set. Once set, carefully remove from the tray or foil and cut into 2.5cm (1in) squares.

Combine the ingredients for the cinnamon sugar in a bowl.

Heat the oil in a deep-fat fryer or wok to 180°C/350°F, or until a tiny piece of the dough browns in 15 seconds. Combine all the ingredients for the batter in a bowl. Dip the cake squares in the batter and deep-fry for 5–6 minutes until golden brown. Drain on kitchen paper, then dip in cinnamon sugar and serve.

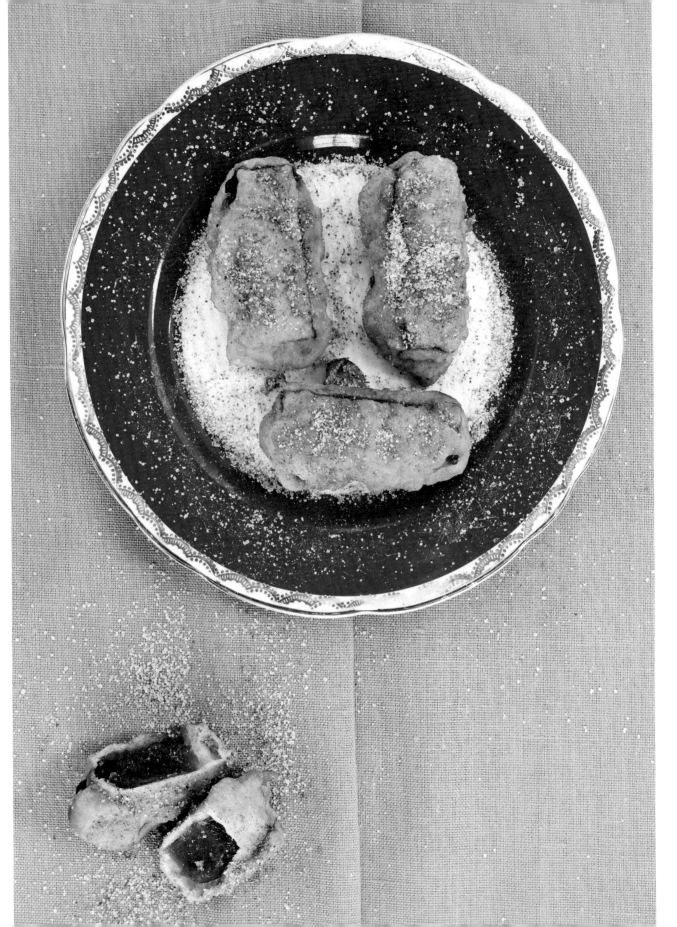

CHONGRING

CHONGQING and the creation of megacities

The term 'megacity' was once applied to cities that had a population in excess of 10 million. But increasingly in Asia, megacities are becoming much more common and much larger. For instance, the Chinese government is planning to create the world's largest megacity by merging nine cities in Guangdong – from Guangzhou in the north to Shenzhen in the south, from Huizhou in the east to Zhaoqing in the west. This will create a metropolis twice the size of Wales with a population of 42 million. The cities lie on the Pearl River Delta, one of the most populous areas in China already, and one of the economic hubs of China. Chongqing has been called a megacity, but it is nothing in comparison.

Chongqing is a major inland city of southwestern China and, administratively, is one of the People's Republic of China's four direct-controlled municipalities (along with Beijing, Shanghai and Tianjin). An ancient and historic city, Chongqing became the provisional capital of the Nationalists under Chiang Kai-shek during the second Sino-Japanese War of 1937–45. The Allies set up their Chinese anti-fascist headquarters there too. The city was heavily bombed by the Japanese, and the population's bravery at this time earned Chongqing the name 'City of Heroes' and a letter of commendation from President Roosevelt. The city was demoted to become a sub-division of Sichuan Province from 1954 to 1997, but it has now regained its previous status. It is probably the world's largest municipality – roughly the size of Austria – and, with a population of over 30 million, has been called China's largest city. This is a misnomer, though, as up until now the population of the core city was very much smaller: the rest of the municipality's population lived in the countryside.

It is a mountainous, modern river city, lying on the upper reaches of the Yangtze: the colour-change confluence of this great river and its tributary, the Jialing, is one of Chongqing's most famous sights. It is the largest inland river port in western China, trading via the Yangtze; following the building of the Three Gorges Dam, and the creation of the great reservoir from the Dam to Chongqing (some 660 kilometres), trading has increased, allowing even seagoing ships from Shanghai, via the Dam's locks, to access western China. Chongqing's population increased too at this time, the city taking in many of the 1.5 million people from over 1,000 towns and villages displaced by the Dam. And with the loss of all that precious agricultural land – a process being echoed all over China as distending cities eat into countryside – I wonder whether this means that China might be losing its ability to feed itself...

And the megacity is still growing. Every day over 1,000 migrants, mainly subsistence farmers, flock in from the country hoping for a new profitable urban life. (This is happening throughout China, and has been called the biggest migration in world history.) Many of them end up as 'bang-bang' men – porters with bamboo poles and ropes who carry goods for others, on their shoulders, up and down the steep hills of

KEN on Chongqing

262

the city. They can be seen everywhere in Chongqing – on street corners and at bus and train stations and piers. It is in megacities like Chongqing that the huge gap between rich and poor, between urban and rural areas, has become most apparent (they say that Chongqing is home to the majority of China's new millionaires). In an effort to address this, amongst other initiatives, Chongqing is subsidising city housing projects, to give homes to many of those flocking in. Chengdu (which could be called the megacity of Sichuan) on the other hand, has focused money and attention on improving life in the surrounding countryside, which sounds more sensible to me.

Whether you are rich or poor, you can eat well in Chongqing. The cuisine is largely an offshoot of Sichuanese cooking, but with a few speciality dishes of its own. The food is perhaps less 'fragrant' that that of Chengdu, and it is certainly hotter. The key ingredient is the special chilli that grows so well throughout Sichuan, around Chongqing, and in neighbouring provinces: the Shizhu or Chaotian red pepper is amongst the spiciest in China (peppers grown in China account for over 50 per cent of world production). The most famously spicy dish of Chongqing is the hotpot, or *malatang* (*ma* and *la* again). Hotpots are known throughout Sichuan, but they were born here, and hotpot restaurants abound. You can go for a regular hotpot, which means choosing a soup base – as hot or bland as you like (or both, in a double pot) – then the vegetables or protein (beef, chicken or pork) you want to cook in that soup. If you fancied duck, frog, rabbit or lamb as the protein content, you might have to opt for a specialist hotpot restaurant. (The locals prefer offal – amply illustrating the axiom that the Chinese will eat anything – and usually choose cow's stomach, penis, intestines, lungs, brain, feet…) After cooking, the items are fished out of the broth and dipped into an array of spicy dips, at its simplest, seasoned sesame oil and chopped garlic. At one time, hotpot was a dish eaten in the depth of winter, but nowadays it is eaten year-round, even in summer – and Chongqing is one of China's four furnace cities, which means it can reach 40°C (104°F) in the summer!

Other dishes you will find locally are bang-bang chicken, stuffed rice dumplings, meat with crispy rice and a pork dish cooked, curiously, with rock sugar. There are the usual street foods on offer, and the same basic flavours as you would find in Sichuan – peppercorns, sesame paste, dofu (tofu), chilli bean sauces, ginger and star anise – although plucked baby chicks on skewers have been seen… The Chongqing people are proud of their cuisine, boasting that it is the best in China. As a result, foreign food chains are not as popular here as they are elsewhere, though efforts are being made to change that: McDonald's serves red bean pie (made with sweetened adzuki bean paste) instead of apple pie, and is actually known mainly for its ice cream. (Desserts are liked in Chongqing, of the sticky rice, wrapped sweet paste, jelly type.) Chongqing food is definitely hotter than in Chengdu, and it is perhaps a little coarser (or so Chengdu people would say), but it is a new, enthusiastic, money-conscious, Westernised city, with a thriving and vital culinary culture.

FLAVOURED OILS

Sichuan pepper oil

Place 225g (8oz) Sichuan peppercorns in a heatproof, sterilised jar. Heat 675ml (1 pint 3fl oz) vegetable oil, then ladle into the jar. Seal and leave for as long as possible to allow the flavours to infuse. To use, drain off the peppercorns.

Chilli oil

Using a pestle and mortar, grind 225g (8oz) small Sichuan chillies very finely. Place in a heatproof, sterilised jar. Heat 675ml (1 pint 3fl oz) vegetable oil, then ladle into the jar. Seal and leave for as long as possible to allow the flavours to infuse. To use, drain off the chillies.

Fragrant oil

Slice a 5cm (2in) piece fresh root ginger and 3 spring onions. Place in a heatproof, sterilised jar with ¼ teaspoon salt. Heat 675ml (1 pint 3fl oz) vegetable oil, then ladle into the jar. Seal and leave for as long as possible to allow the flavours to infuse.

GLOSSARY

Adzuki red bean paste
Adzuki beans are small, dull-red and slightly square in shape. They are high in protein. Sweet red bean paste is made by boiling the beans, then mashing to a paste and cooking until dry. It is a popular filling for Chinese desserts, buns and cakes.

Bai jiou
This is a clear, white spirit, distilled from grain. Use in marinades or pickles, or drinks.

Bamboo shoots
The young shoots of the bamboo tree, usually found vacuum-packed or in tins or jars. Pickled sour bamboo shoots are prepared by pickling boiled bamboo sprouts in brine, giving them a sour taste. They are also pickled in chilli oil, giving them a spicy taste. Bamboo shoots add a crunchy texture to salads, soups, stir-fries and braised dishes.

Bean curd – see Dofu

Chilli bean paste
This hot sauce is made from black beans and chopped chillies that have been fermented with salt. Some versions include fermented soya beans, garlic and other spices. Good in soups, braised dishes and sauces. Use with caution, as some varieties are extremely hot.

Chilli oil
This is made by infusing crushed dried red chillies in hot oil to give an intensely hot, clear, red oil. Some chilli oils also contain specks of dried chillies. Use in sauces, stuffings and soups. (See page opposite)

Chilli sauce
Made from chillies, vinegar, sugar and salt, this bright red, hot sauce can be used in cooking, or as a dipping sauce. There are several varieties, some flavoured with garlic and vinegar.

Chinese aubergine
Pale-purple in colour, this is longer and more slender than the European variety and has a more delicate flavour, but can be used in the same way. Bake, fry, grill or braise.

Chinese cabbage (Chinese leaf)
This cabbage has a mild taste and delicate aroma. The white stalks retain their crunchy texture when cooked. Use as a vegetable, or in soups and stir-fries.

Chinese chives (garlic chives)
These have long, flat, green leaves and a strong garlic flavour. There are three varieties: yellow, the mildest; flowering, with small, edible yellow flowers; and green, with the strongest flavour. The flowers can be eaten. Use them in soups, stuffings and stir-fries.

Chinese cinnamon bark/stick
True cinnamon is the dried bark of the cinnamon tree. It is available as thin, rolled cinnamon sticks, which have a concentrated, robust flavour, or as bark, whose aromatic flavour is good in braised dishes.

Chinese dried citrus (orange/tangerine) peel
A strongly aromatic alternative to fresh citrus zest, with a pleasant smell, but slightly bitter taste. Rehydrate in water or rice wine before using. It is most often used in savoury braised or simmered dishes, and occasionally in stir-fries.

Chinese dried tree ear fungus – see Mushrooms, Cloud ear (tree ear) fungus

Chinese dried wood ear fungus – see Mushrooms, Chinese dried wood ear fungus

Chinese five-spice powder
This distinctive seasoning is a blend of cinnamon, cloves, Sichuan peppercorns, fennel and star anise, which give it the sour, bitter, pungent, sweet and salty flavours of Chinese cooking. Use sparingly for braised meats and in marinades.

Chinese leaf – see Chinese cabbage

Chinese rock sugar
This is a solid mixture of refined and semi-refined sugar with large, slightly golden-yellow crystals. If necessary, crush the lumps into smaller pieces. Use for sauces, syrups and glazes. Use half the quantity of soft brown sugar as a substitute. Red rock sugar is refined from red sugar cane.

Chinese rose liqueur wine
Made from sorghum wine and distilled with rose petals, sugar and salt, Chinese rose wine is predominantly a cooking wine, but can be used in drinks. Clear in colour and slightly salty in taste, it has a very subtle rose fragrance. Use in marinades and roasts, or in a cocktail.

Chinese water spinach
Similar to European spinach, this has green, supple leaves and hollow stems that absorb spices well and remain crunchy after cooking. Use in stir-fries and soups.

Chinkiang black rice vinegar – see Vinegar, Chinese black rice vinegar

Cloud ear (tree ear) fungus – see Mushrooms, Cloud ear (tree ear) fungus

Dofu (tofu)
Made from yellow soya beans, this protein-rich curd comes in various forms, including firm, extra firm (pressed), silken and soft. Although quite bland, it takes on the flavour of whatever ingredients it is cooked with. The firmer varieties are used for stir-fries, soups and grilling.

Deep-fried dofu are cubes of fresh dofu that have been deep-fried until the surface is crisp and golden, with a little soft curd remaining inside. Can be eaten on its own with dipping sauces, added to braised dishes, or used as a topping to give texture and protein.

Dofu-gan is dry and extra firm. Often vacuum-packed, it is available plain or braised with flavouring.

Dofu ru (or fermented dofu) is dofu that has been preserved in rice wine, brine or with chillies and condiments. Often sold cubed, it comes in white and red varieties in many flavours and is quite strong in flavour. It can be eaten on its own or used as a marinade, condiment or an accompaniment to congee. It can also be used to flavour braised dishes or vegetables.

Soft and silken dofu have a cream cheese-like texture and can be used in a variety of dishes. Silken dofu crumbles easily and can be used in sauces and desserts to give a creamy texture.

Dried chillies/flakes
Crushed dried whole red chillies, with their seeds, give a fiery heat when added to dishes, so are best used with some caution. At home, you can grind whole dried chillies in a pestle and mortar to give flakes, which can then be added to dishes.

Dried lily stems (buds)
Dried lily buds are yellow-gold in color, with a musky or earthy taste. Use in soups and stir-fries. To use, soak in warm water for about 20 minutes to soften them before cooking.

Dried shrimp
Orange-red in colour and very pungent, these are cooked shrimp that have been dried and salted to preserve them. They are used as a seasoning, or in soups to add flavour and texture. To use, soak in hot water for 20 minutes to soften them before cooking.

Edamame beans

High in protein, these are green soya beans, harvested while the pods are still attached to the bush. The pods are cooked whole and the beans are then squeezed out. They can be eaten as a vegetable in their own right or added to other dishes to give texture.

Fermented black beans

These small black soya beans have been cooked and fermented with salt and spices, giving them a salty, pungent taste, rich aroma and soft texture. Often used as a seasoning or in steamed, braised and stir-fried dishes.

Fermented cabbage

Finely shredded raw cabbage is mixed with salt, water, vinegar and sugar, then tightly packed into an airtight container and left to ferment, which preserves the cabbage and gives it a tangy taste. Can be used in stews and braises, or combined with other ingredients with rice.

Fermented dofu – see Dofu

Five-spice powder – see Chinese five-spice powder

Garlic chives – see Chinese chives

Goji berry (Chinese wolfberry)

The deep-red, dried fruit of an evergreen shrub, these are a similar size to a raisin. Sweet and nutritionally rich, they can be eaten raw or cooked.

Hoisin sauce

A thick, dark, brownish-red sauce, whose basic ingredients are fermented soya beans, salt, starch, spices and sweeteners. Sugar, garlic, vinegar and chillies are also common ingredients. Use as a condiment, glaze, marinade or dipping sauce.

Jasmine rice

An aromatic rice with slender, long grains, this white rice originates from Thailand. When cooked it is soft, white and fluffy. Use as an accompaniment to dishes.

Long Jing tea

A mild green (unfermented) tea with a sweet flavour and pure aroma. It is high in antioxidants and contains vitamin C and amino acids. In cooking, use as a flavouring.

Lotus leaves

A popular ingredient in Chinese medicine, these leaves can be used to wrap ingredients before cooking. Cut to size and then soak in hot water before use, according to the recipe. The leaves themselves are not eaten.

Lotus root

This is the root of the lotus flower that grows underwater and is available fresh (vacuum-packed), dried or in tins. Fresh lotus root should be peeled before use. When cut, the interior has a distinctive lacy appearance. The texture is slightly crunchy and mildly sweet. The root can be eaten raw, in salads, or on its own with dips, as well as cooked in many different dishes.

Lychee

A small, oval fruit with a spiny red skin, the lychee is the fruit of an evergreen tree native to southern China. The flesh is translucent white or pink with an aromatic and distinctive flavour. Each fruit contains a single, large, shiny black seed. Available fresh or tinned, they are usually served as a dessert.

Malt sugar (maltose)

A thick, treacle-like ingredient made from fermented barley. Usually diluted with water or vinegar and used as a glaze.

MUSHROOMS

Cloud ear (tree ear) fungus

Smaller and more tender than wood ears, cloud ears are sold mainly in dried form. Quite bland, they soak up the flavour of whatever they are cooked with. Their crunchy texture is useful in soups and stir-fries. To use, soak in hot water for 20 minutes – they will puff up like clouds.

Chinese dried black mushrooms

Available in various sizes and shades of brown, these mushrooms add flavour and aroma to dishes, while absorbing sauces and spices. To use, soak in hot water for 20 minutes to soften them before cooking. Their slightly salty taste complements savoury dishes well.

Chinese dried wood ear fungus

A larger variety of the cloud ear fungus, these dark brown-black fungi do not impart flavour but add colour and crispness to any dish. To use, soak in hot water for 20 minutes – they will swell to four or five times their size.

Shiitake mushrooms (fresh and dried)

These nutrient-rich, large dark-brown mushrooms are umbrella-shaped fungi that are prized for their culinary and medicinal properties. To use the dried variety, soak in water for 20 minutes to soften slightly before cooking. Use in soups, stir-fries, steamed or simmered dishes.

Nian Gao

These are sticky cakes made from glutinous rice, and thought to bring good fortune when eaten during Chinese New Year. They can be flavoured or plain.

NOODLES

Egg noodles

Made from wheat flour, egg yolk and salt, these are the most common type of noodle and come in various shapes and thicknesses. They are available fresh or dried.

Mung bean (transparent/cellophane) noodles

These transparent noodles are made from the starch of green mung beans and water. They come in various thicknesses, vermicelli being the thinnest type. To use, soak in hot water for 5–6 minutes to soften them before cooking. If using in soups or deep-frying, no pre-soaking is necessary. They become translucent when cooked. Use in salads, soups, braised dishes and stir-fries. They can also be deep-fried and used as a garnish.

Vermicelli rice noodles

Dried rice noodles come in many widths and varieties. Vermicelli are a fine, creamy-coloured noodle. To use, soak in hot water for 5 minutes to soften them before cooking. If using in salads, soak for 20 minutes. No need to soak if using them in a soup. They turn opaque when cooked. Use in soups, salads and stir-fries. They can also be deep-fried, when they expand and become light and crisp.

Wheat flour noodles

These noodles originated in the north of China, where wheat is a staple crop. Made from wheat flour and water, they are available fresh or dried. Use in soups, salads and stir-fries.

Oyster sauce

A richly flavoured, thick brown sauce made from dried oysters, soy sauce and other seasonings. Use as a seasoning, in marinades, and to add flavour and colour to braised and stir-fried dishes and vegetables. Use with caution as it is very salty. Vegetarian oyster sauce, made from mushrooms, is also available.

Pak choy

With fleshy white stalks and broad green leaves, this vegetable can be boiled, steamed or stir-fried.

Pickled chilli bamboo shoots – see Bamboo shoots

Potato flour
This gluten-free flour is made from steamed, dried and ground potatoes. The silky smooth flour gives a wonderful crispness to ingredients when they are coated in it before being shallow- or deep-fried. It has stronger binding properties than cornflour, but cornflour can be used as a substitute.

Preserved mustard greens
The leaves of mustard cabbage are pickled with water, vinegar, chilli, salt and sugar. Use as a vegetable, in soups, or as a flavouring ingredient.

Sesame oil – see Toasted sesame oil

Sesame paste
Made from crushed, roasted white sesame seeds blended with toasted sesame oil, this golden brown paste is used with other sauces as a flavouring. It gives a nutty taste to marinades and can be used in both hot and cold dishes. Tahini can be used as a substitute, but it is lighter in flavour and so you will need to add more toasted sesame oil.

Sesame seeds
These seeds, with a nutty flavour and high oil content, add taste and texture to many dishes. They are available in black, white/yellow and red varieties, toasted and untoasted.

Shaoxing rice wine
Made from rice, millet and yeast, this wine is aged for anything between three and twenty years, sometimes longer. It is used for both drinking and cooking. When added while cooking meat or fish it removes the odour or rawness and gives a bittersweet finish. It is used in marinades, stir-fries, braised and simmered dishes. Dry sherry makes a good substitute.

Sichuan chillies
These come in many varieties, both fresh and dried, the most common being a short, fat, bright red chilli that is hot and fragrant.

Sichuan peppercorns
These are the dried berries of a shrub and are widely used all over China. They have a sharp taste and lemony fragrance and can be roasted, cooked in oil to flavour the oil, or mixed with salt as a condiment for any dish.

SOY SAUCE

Dark soy sauce
Made from fermented soya beans and a roasted grain (usually wheat), dark soy sauce is left to age for longer than light soy sauce. Less salty in taste and slightly thicker than light soy, it is used in marinades, sauces, stews and braised dishes to give flavour and colour.

Light soy sauce
Made from fermented soya beans and wheat, light soy sauce is aged for less time than the dark variety and is saltier in flavour. It can be used in soups, stir-fries and braised and stewed dishes. Wheat-free (tamari) and Low-sodium varieties are available.

Spring roll wrappers/pastry
Made from flour, salt and water, these paper-thin skins are used for wrapping foods, such as in spring rolls, before deep-frying. They can also be eaten raw, filled with salad and dressings. They are available fresh or frozen. Filo pastry makes a good substitute.

Star anise
A staple ingredient in Chinese cooking, star anise is the star-shaped seed pod of a small tree that grows in southwest China. Similar in flavour to aniseed, although more robust, it is one of the ingredients of Chinese five-spice powder, and is used in braised dishes.

Thousand-year-old eggs
These are eggs (usually duck) that have been buried in clay, ash, salt and lime, then left to mature for a few weeks to a few months, depending on the process. The yolk turns semi-solid, with a grey to green colour, while the white becomes a brown, jelly-like substance. They have a strong smell and a love-it or loathe-it taste. To use, rinse under water, then peel off the outer layer and shell. Serve as an appetiser, in soups or congee, with dofu or rice, or as a condiment.

Toasted sesame oil
Made from crushed and toasted white sesame seeds, this dark-coloured, thick, aromatic oil is used as a flavouring or seasoning. It is not suitable for use as a cooking oil since it burns easily. The flavour is intense, so use sparingly.

Tofu – see Dofu

Tree ears – see Mushrooms, Cloud ear (tree ear) fungus

Vermicelli mung bean noodles – see Noodles, Mung bean noodles

VINEGAR

Chinese black rice vinegar
This rich, aromatic vinegar is used in braised dishes and sauces, and with noodles. When cooked, it gives dishes a smoky flavour with a mellow and earthy taste. Balsamic vinegar makes a good substitute.

Plain (white) rice vinegar
Clear and mild, this vinegar is used in dressings, as a seasoning and for pickling. Cider vinegar can be used as a substitute.

Red rice vinegar
This clear, pale red vinegar has a slightly sweet and salty flavour. It is used for dipping sauces and in sweet and sour dishes.

Water chestnuts
Water chestnuts, the roots of an aquatic plant, are available fresh, in vacuum packs, or tinned (but these have an inferior taste to fresh). They resemble a chestnut in shape and colouring and have a firm, crunchy texture. Can be used in salads, fillings and stir-fries.

Wheat flour dumpling wrappers/skins
Made from wheat flour, salt and water, these flat, thin discs of dough are used to make dumplings. They are available fresh or frozen. When using, keep covered with a damp towel to prevent them from drying.

Wheat flour noodles – see Noodles

Wheat starch
A finely textured white powder obtained from wheat grain. It is combined with hot water and rolled out to make dumpling skins, which turn from opaque to translucent once steamed.

Wonton wrapper
Made from egg, wheat flour, salt and water, wonton wrappers are used to make dumplings. Available fresh or frozen.

Wood ear mushrooms – see Mushrooms, Chinese dried wood ear fungus

Yellow bean sauce
A thick, spicy, aromatic sauce made from fermented yellow soya beans, dark brown sugar and rice wine. There are two forms: whole bean sauce, and mashed or puréed beans. Use in marinades and as a flavouring in many savoury dishes.

WITH THANKS FROM KEN

I begin with Ching, my partner in crime. She has been so terrific, a real trooper and I am delighted to have taken this journey with her. I not only learnt a lot from her but also shared so much laughter and good food. We are now life-long friends.

Of course, I owe a tremendous debt to Keo Films, especially to Paula, as well as her team and Jade in particular. Our filming crew was exceptional and I take a bow to: Emma, James, Craig, Qiao, Torch, Lillian, Daisy, Chef Kai and Daniel. Mr. Zhao was wonderful and exceptionally helpful.

Lee not only tested the recipes for me but gave me critical comments. Muna and Joe expertly guided the book while Susan assisted us with the introductions. Of course, my agents, Julian and Carole - their advice and counsel was, as always, invaluable.

But my biggest gratitude is to all the chefs and families who opened up their homes and kitchens to us with a generosity that touched my heart. I am forever grateful.

WITH THANKS FROM CHING

To the powers at BBC, thank your for such an amazing experience – this is one I will treasure for the rest of my life. I feel so privileged to have had this opportunity to experience modern China and delve further into my culinary heritage. Heartfelt and sincere thanks to Janice Hadlow, Tom Edwards and all who championed this project at the BBC.

Cooking, filming and writing this book whilst travelling in China, was not without its challenges. I am indebted to these professionals who made getting up at the crack of dawn and finishing at the crack of dawn easier to stomach – Paula Trafford (for your support from day 1), Emma Peach (Panda 1) (for your passion and determination), James Nutt (Panda 2)(you are a talented nutcase), India Bourke, Catia di Giorgio, Jade Miller Robinson, Craig Hastings (for your humour), Daniel (for your care), Daisy Newton Dunn, Mr.Zhao, Lillian Chen, Qiao Xin, Liu Kai, Torch.

Thank you to everyone at Random House for making this book such a pleasure to work on. Thank you to Muna Reyal, Joe Cottington, Susan Fleming, Liz and Max Haarala Hamilton and Katie Giovanni for a gorgeous book despite the tight deadlines!

Thanks to Katie Rice, Jamie Coleman, Zaria Rich for convincing me to challenge myself! To Toby Eady, Michael Foster and Michael Kagan for making it happen. To Agatha Chapman Poole, thanks for your support back in the UK during my travels abroad.

To all the cooks we encountered in China – thank you for your warmth and generous spirit – for sharing your delicious food and passion with an open heart, I am forever grateful and humbled by the stories you all shared, they touched me and nourished me, both spiritually and emotionally, more than you know. I will cherish our exchanges, however fleeting, for the rest of my life.

To Ken, my 'sifu' - I salute you with heartfelt thanks with a bottle of the finest Chateau La Fete! You have carried the torch for us Chinese living in the West, representing us, sharing your knowledge with the West with great passion, graciousness, humour and authority. Your lifelong dedication and the challenges you faced throughout your professional years couldn't have been easy. You are a true leader and culinary master. I am so honoured to have shared this incredible journey with you.

Thanks to all my friends and family. To Jamie Cho, thanks for always being there through the good and bad.To my mum and dad, thank you for forcing me to go to Chinese Sunday school all those years ago when I was growing up. Rusty Mandarin did come in handy…

Finally, this is for my grandmother and grandfather – for the hardships you endured and the sacrifices you made in order to give us a better life.

10 9 8 7 6 5 4 3 2 1

This book is published to accompany a television series, produced by Keo Films and first broadcast on BBC2 in 2012.

Executive producer: Paula Trafford
Series producer: Emma Peach
Commissioning executive for the BBC: Tom Edwards

Published in 2012 by BBC Books, an imprint of Ebury Publishing. A Random House Group company.

© Keo Films 2012
© Promo Group Limited 2012
© Ching-He Huang 2012

All photography © Woodlands Books Ltd 2012, unless specified below

Ken Hom and Ching-He Huang have asserted their right to be identified as the authors of this work.

The Random House Group Limited Reg. No. 954009

Addresses for companies within the Random House Group can be found at www.randomhouse.co.uk

A CIP catalogue record for this book is available from the British Library.

ISBN 978 1 849 90498 8

The Random House Group Limited supports The Forest Stewardship Council (FSC®), the leading international forest certification organisation. Our books carrying the FSC label are printed on FSC® certified paper. FSC is the only forest certification scheme endorsed by the leading environmental organisations, including Greenpeace. Our paper procurement policy can be found at www.randomhouse.co.uk/environment

Commissioning editor: Muna Reyal
Project editor: Joe Cottington
Copy editor: Barbara Dixon
Editor: Susan Fleming
Designer: Pene Parker
Food photography: Haarala Hamilton
Food stylist: Katie Giovanni
Location photography: Craig Hastings

Photographs on p88–89 © View Stock/Alamy; p260–261 © Lou Linwei/Alamy; p130 (top left and middle right), p131 (top left and bottom left), p242 (top left) © Ching-He Huang

Colour origination by AltaImage
Printed and bound by Firmengruppe APPL, aprinta druck, Wemding, Germany

To buy books by your favourite authors and register for offers, visit www.randomhouse.co.uk

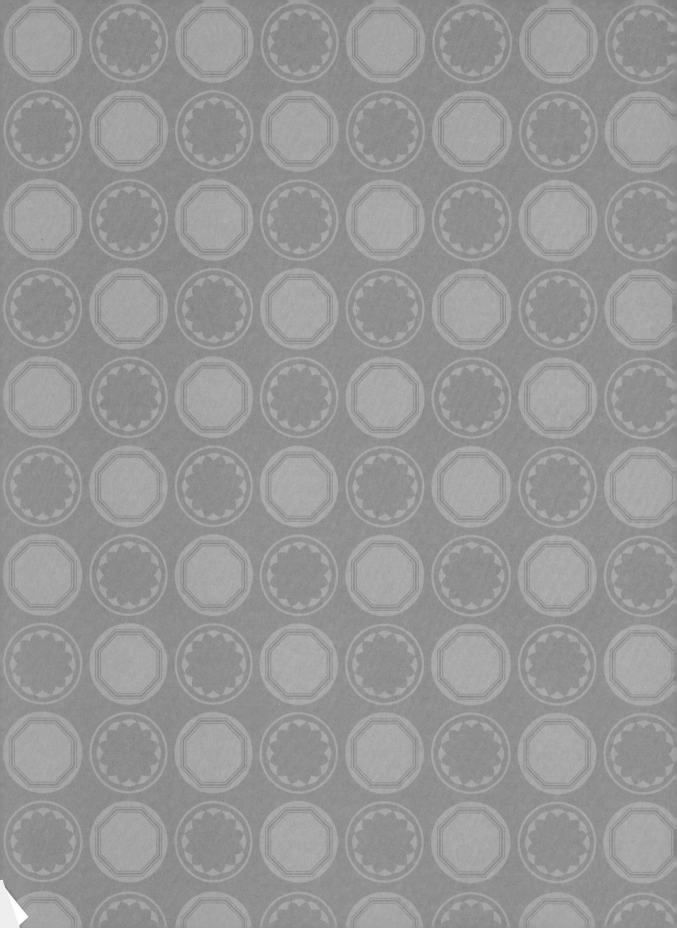